Reverse De
Final Fantasy VII

Reverse Design Series

Author
Patrick Holleman

Series Titles

Reverse Design: Final Fantasy VI

Reverse Design: Chrono Trigger

Reverse Design: Super Mario World

Reverse Design: Half-Life

Reverse Design: Final Fantasy VII

Reverse Design: Diablo II

Reverse Design
Final Fantasy VII

Patrick Holleman

CRC Press
Taylor & Francis Group
Boca Raton London New York

CRC Press is an imprint of the
Taylor & Francis Group, an **informa** business

CRC Press
Taylor & Francis Group
6000 Broken Sound Parkway NW, Suite 300
Boca Raton, FL 33487-2742

© 2019 by Taylor & Francis Group, LLC
CRC Press is an imprint of Taylor & Francis Group, an Informa business

No claim to original U.S. Government works

Printed on acid-free paper

International Standard Book Number-13: 978-1-1383-2410-7 (Paperback)
978-1-1383-2477-0 (Hardback)

Library of Congress Cataloging-in-Publication Data

Names: Holleman, Patrick, author.
Title: Reverse design : Final Fantasy VII / Patrick Holleman.
Description: Boca Raton : Taylor & Francis, 2018. | Includes
bibliographical references.
Identifiers: LCCN 2018021677| ISBN 9781138324770 (hardback : alk. paper) |
ISBN 9781138324107 (paperback : alk. paper)
Subjects: LCSH: Final fantasy VII. | Computer games--Design. |
Fantasy games--Design.
Classification: LCC GV1469.35.F4 H65 2018 | DDC 794.8--dc23
LC record available at https://lccn.loc.gov/2018021677

Visit the Taylor & Francis Web site at
http://www.taylorandfrancis.com

and the CRC Press Web site at
http://www.crcpress.com

Contents

Introduction

This is the *Reverse Design* for *Final Fantasy VII*, the fifth entry in the *Reverse Design* Series. The goal of the series has been to reverse-engineer all of the game design decisions that went into classic games. Before this entry, I published books on *Final Fantasy VI*, *Chrono Trigger*, *Super Mario World*, and *Half-Life*. You do not need to have read any of those books in order to understand this one, although the entry on *Final Fantasy VI* makes for a good point of comparison. This is because many of the historical trends expressed by *Final Fantasy VI* continue, and indeed culminate, in *Final Fantasy VII*. (Hereafter, I shorten the title of all the Final Fantasy games to the traditional "*FF*," (except at the beginning of a sentence). Everything you really need to know about this game or the history of the Japanese role-playing game (JRPG) will be recapitulated in the early sections of this book.

The principal challenge in writing about *FFVII* is that it is one of the most-criticized videogames in the history of the medium. From the time it came out until the present day, critics have considered the merits and failures of *FFVII* time and again. Admirers of the game have defended it for almost two decades. Critics have poked holes in the game and in what they perceive to be the game-playing public's nostalgia for it. Many writers still feel a remarkable ambivalence about the game. That is, they can't make up their minds about the game, but they're still writing about it even now. Such a mixed field of criticism makes the writing of this book somewhat different than the writing of any of the previous *Reverse Designs*, which were all about games that are classics by consensus. My task in this book is to explain why *FFVII* was a classic game because of its game design ideas, but I won't try to persuade you to like it. I do not believe in persuasion, as such. Rather, I believe the only honest and upright way to change someone's opinion about a subject is to reveal that subject more fully, and let that other person reconsider their opinion in the light of that revelation. This is exactly what I intend to do for

FFVII, for I believe that critics on all sides (positive, negative, and ambivalent) have not seen the game for all that it truly is.

There are three criticisms that have typified the negative perception of *FFVII* that I feel are important to address. The first and oldest criticism is that there is too much story and too many cutscenes and the game is boring as a result. Because it uses so many of these cutscenes, *FFVII* was once a lightning rod for critics who thought games should eschew storytelling. Thankfully, this criticism is mostly obsolete because dozens (if not hundreds) of games have since surpassed *FFVII* in regards to story, cutscenes, and other non-interactive forms of content. Some critics still do not like it for this reason, but now it is clear that such an objection is a matter of taste and not really worth debating. The second typical criticism is that the game is too simple and/or too easy. Critics point out that *FFVII* has been denuded of all the interesting tactical choices that are present in games like *Pokémon*, *Shin Megami Tensei*, or even *Final Fantasy V*. *Final Fantasy VII* is not a particularly hard game, but in Chapter 3 of this book, I will explain how *FFVII* didn't get rid of complexity and difficulty—it simply moved those things to a place in the game where players don't necessarily notice or expect them. Indeed, the decision to do this is very important in the historical context of the JRPG. The third typical criticism of *FFVII* is that its plot and characters are juvenile. Some critics say that *FFVII* was originally popular because it appealed to an immature audience through immature themes. By tapping into the "teen angst" of its audience, it cemented its place in the audience's memory in the same way that bad, old pop songs do. This is the most easily rebutted criticism and the one that I will address first.

Final Fantasy VII tells a story about survivors. To use a bit more nuance, it tells a story about characters who have outlived the people, places, and things that gave them their identities. Most of the characters in *FFVII* are motivated by the loss of something that once defined who they were. The loss of something—usually a loved one or a hometown—is a common motivation for videogame characters. It's something that prompts them to seek revenge, and that revenge gives structure to a violent game. This kind of motivation can often come across as very lowbrow. Everyone understands the motivation for revenge because it is one of the petty, hasty, and emotional reactions we have all felt from the time that we were children. Since everyone knows from personal experience how childish and base those emotions are, many videogames come across as inauthentic and shallow. *Final Fantasy VII* isn't just a story of revenge, however. The story it tells is, at times, a deconstruction of a revenge story. Some of the characters appear to be seeking revenge, and indeed they sometimes even fool themselves into believing they are, but we'll see in Chapter 2 of this book (characters and their motivations) how the *FFVII* team dismantles the idea of revenge in an insightful way. With that in mind, I do want to give a brief example of the point I'm trying to make.

Barret Wallace is the easiest example to use in illustrating the theme of tragic survivorship in *FFVII*. Barret was a coal miner in the town of Corel until Shinra Inc. arrived and made coal obsolete. Rising tensions between the former coal miners and Shinra led to the slaughter of the townsfolk and the destruction of the town. Barret, an important figure in a coal mining town, reacts to the loss of his identity by becoming a militant environmental activist. This unlikely change of career captures the wonderfully imperfect ways in which all the *FFVII* characters deal with the loss of their identities. Several characters remark how badly Mako energy damages the world in which *FFVII* takes place, but presumably coal (if it is anything like its real world counterpart) is quite environmentally damaging as well. In the 20th century, Japan was beset by serious pollution problems, and so there is simply no way that the writers of *FFVII* didn't know what coal mines and coal power plants do to the environment. Having a survivor of a coal mining town become an environmental extremist is a deeply ironic and totally intentional move on the part of the writers. Indeed, Cait Sith points out that Barret's crusade is not nearly as noble as he imagines it.

In a later scene (also taking place on the airship), Barret comes to realize that his true goal was much more personal and much less political than he originally claimed, and that revenge was never the right motivation.

Beneath the idealism and the violence that are products of his pain, Barret's real goal is to safeguard the life of the only connection he has to his past and to his identity: his daughter, Marlene.

Final Fantasy VII's central theme is not about growing up. If anything, it's the opposite: it's about characters who are left behind with no meaningful identity after the world changes. All but one of the main characters behave the way that

Barret does, by desperately clinging to the last remaining fragment of their old identities. I'll cover each character's particular relation to the theme in Chapter 2, but I want to make a point here about the maturity of this idea. This is a problem which only adults can have: one must have a firm sense of identity for the loss of that identity to be a problem. The resilience of children means that they can quickly form new identities while they are still young, and avoid this. How many teenagers can properly understand how Marlene represents everything meaningful in Barret's past and future? How many of them can understand what it means for Cid to strive his whole life for a single career goal of going into space, only to have to give it up, apparently forever? How many students in junior high school can understand how Tifa has to keep a violent, unstable, compulsive liar in her life, because otherwise she has no tangible connection to the majority of her past experiences? Maybe there are a few young people who have had enough misfortune to experience these things, but I doubt that any of those few have really processed and understood those experiences yet. The original audience of *FFVII* interpreted—one might even say allegorized—the message of the game to be about themselves and their struggle to grow up. I would never deny an audience the right to see the high drama of a fictional narrative as a metaphor for their own lives. That is the very essence of catharsis. Nevertheless, *FFVII* is a game made by adults, and it reflects adult anxieties and concerns.

The Structure of This Book

The thematic material in *FFVII* would not be very interesting if it were not also reflected in the design of the game. The story that *FFVII* tells is one of characters who have outlived the contexts they grew up in, and who therefore struggle to find a place in the new world. The designers of *FFVII* had a similar problem. The original RPG, *Dungeons & Dragons* (hereafter *D&D*), was so massive and so artistically complete that designers who came later had trouble doing something truly original within the genre. Like many popular series, *Final Fantasy* started off as something like a simplified *D&D* campaign with a few small modifications. Only so many games like that could exist in one market, however, and so the *Final Fantasy* team—like many RPG design teams—had to struggle to find a new voice for their game in a rapidly changing environment. This struggle is a fascinating one, and it explains why *FFVII* is so different from the RPGs that are popular today.

In Chapter 1 of this book, we'll trace the lineage of *FFVII* by going all the way back to the beginning and seeing how RPG designers employed three different strategies for dealing with the titanic influence of *D&D*. Although we'll look at all three strategies, *FFVII* is a great example of just one of them—the strategy of specialization. This strategy explains why *FFVII* became focused on storytelling, characterization and world-building at the expense of traditional RPG ideas like class systems and tactical combat.

In Chapter 2 of this book, we'll see how the character design in *FFVII* reflects the central thematic concern in a variety of ways. All but one of the player characters are driven by the loss of something that gave them their identity. What's more, the antagonists (Rufus and Sephiroth) actually embody two villainous extremes of identity, context and survivorship. I want to be clear that at no point will I actually try to defend *FFVII's* script as a literary achievement. Its prose is not of an especially high caliber in either English or Japanese. That said, character design is an aspect of RPGs that goes back to the very beginnings of the genre, and I think that *FFVII* is artistically great in that regard. The really interesting thing about *FFVII's* character designs is how they're clearly driven by game design ideas. Each of the main characters in the game is the result of the same process that a game designer would use to fill a platformer or shooter level with content. Thus, we can study these characters not just as fictitious people, but also as artifacts of a game design process which transcends genres.

In Chapter 3, we'll also look at the actual word-for-word how of the script by comparison with other texts both in the *Final Fantasy* series and outside of it. Although *FFVII's* language is not especially expressive or rich in metaphor (at least not most of the time), it is often judicious and works as a template for how to tell a certain kind of story in a certain kind of game. One of the ways we can understand the intent of the creators of *FFVII* is to look at the script of the game in comparison to earlier entries in the series. This examination shows us that story became an increasingly important part of the project's vision and voice. As a point of comparison, I will compare the statistical analysis of the text of *FFVII* to the same analysis performed on the text of the classic American novel, *The Great Gatsby*. The comparison between the two reveals some useful points about the structure of conflict in novels and videogames, specifically in the way that conflict in those different media is portrayed. The eBook version of this text also contains the same analysis performed on the game's thousand-plus NPCs, with a large discussion about the practical use of NPCs in RPGs generally.

Chapter 4 of this book examines the way that difficulty in *FFVII* is structured. *Final Fantasy VII* has been criticized for being easy and simple. It is a fairly easy game, but it is far from being simple. The game can be divided into four phases, all of which have a different design principle that shapes the challenge in that phase. Those phases are: introduction, abundant inconvenience, damage racing, and level acceleration. In each case, the player has to contend with a qualitatively different set of enemy behaviors that shape the experience of the game at the whole-dungeon level.

Chapter 5 of this book goes on to examine the greater challenges and complexity of phase four, and how the real challenge of *FFVII* is in exploiting the game's many interlocking level-up systems. Although the *Final Fantasy* team had to strip away many of the traditional elements of the RPG in order to make the game they wanted, they didn't merely leave holes in their game. Indeed, they added quite a bit to their game, but in ways that weren't totally orthodox at the time or obvious to the casual observer. Thus, phase four is the best place to find and understand complexity as it exists in *FFVII*.

Chapter 6 adds to Chapters 4 and 5 by outlining the six important archetypes of enemies found in the game. Most enemies in *FFVII* fall into one of these six categories that describe their behavior and a range of stats they tend to have. There's still a large variety of battles that can be composed from these, and even enemies in the same archetype group are not exactly the same. Nevertheless, there are patterns among these enemies that show us what the designers were thinking of when they set out to make the hundreds of encounters the game has to offer. The eBook version of this text also contains a significant statistical analysis of these types, and also addresses types of enemies that fall outside (sometimes only a little bit outside) normal type definitions.

Chapter 7 explains the construction of towns and dungeons. The design of maps largely confirms what we see elsewhere in the game—that the focus of the developers was on creating a persuasive world first, and on using typical town and dungeon structures second. This isn't uniformly true, but there are lots of examples of the trend being true in *FFVII*. Moreover, there are a few surprises not just in the way that maps are constructed artistically, but how they are filled with loot and enemies. Although it's not easy to sense it all the time, the random encounter rate for the game is fine-tuned to allow the developers to use maps for storytelling purposes. The distribution of loot in dungeons also has story-related causes in significant places, although overall it follows a fairly traditional RPG pattern. In general, we'll see how towns and dungeons create a sense of place while still affording the kind of gameplay that keeps players engaged through loot and battles.

Chapter 8 analyzes the music of *FFVII* with special regard to the structure, length and purpose of the music. Nobuo Uematsu, the composer for *FFVII*, was a pioneer in musical techniques idiosyncratic to the videogame form. One of his techniques was a non-repeating introduction which—although used by his contemporaries—is developed in surprising ways in *Final Fantasies VI* through *VIII*. The introduction of seamless cinema-to-gameplay transitions forces a change in the structure of individual tracks in *FFVII* and the score as a whole, as compared to earlier titles. The purpose of these tracks changes in meaningful ways as well. The central focus of the design in *FFVI* was on the large roster of characters, and the score reflects this clearly. In *FFVII*, the focus of the game has changed significantly and so the use or purpose of each track has changed accordingly. Because the relation of characters to places is such an important part of the game's main theme, the score emphasizes place over character. We'll take a look at all of those things in a statistical fashion to see the differences between *FFVII* and its predecessor and successor.

Final Fantasy VII and the History of RPGs

Final Fantasy VII is a role-playing game, and so in one sense it is relatively easy to write about it. Role-playing games (RPGs) are probably more popular now than they have ever been, and that familiarity makes the audience for this book a little larger and a little more familiar with its technical terms. On the other hand, there is a lot of disagreement in the RPG audience about what RPGs should be. If a player's first experiences with an RPG are in games like *Skyrim*, *The Witcher*, or *Dragon Age*—or older games like *Ultima*, *Wizardry*, or *Baldur's Gate*—then that player might have certain expectations of an RPG. The games I just mentioned feature lots of non-linear/open-world exploration, branching dialogue, character classes, deep character customization, and the ability to make decisions that meaningfully shape the narrative. *Final Fantasy VII*, by contrast, is linear, authorial, has no meaningful character classes (with one exception), minimal character customization, and no way to meaningfully change the outcome of the narrative. That's a pretty profound discrepancy in style, which begs two questions: why do many RPGs have all those features I listed, and why does *FFVII* lack them? The answer to these questions isn't as simple as developer preference. It isn't as simple as saying "well, *FFVII* came from Japan." To understand the real reason why *FFVII* differs from the most popular RPGs of our era, we have to go all the way back to the first RPG, *Dungeons & Dragons*, and see how its influence caused designers to make a variety of very strange games.

One of the best and most helpful things about the history of RPGs is that it has a clear starting point. The RPG from which all others are descended is *Dungeons & Dragons* (traditionally called "*D&D*," an abbreviation that I will use except at the beginning of a sentence). The history of videogames is not quite so clear; many different developers started creating games at different times and in different places, and videogames didn't find their unique voice for several years after they became a mass market product. *Dungeons & Dragons* took shape in just a few years, and then continually expanded. By 1981, the year in which computer RPGs began to appear in significant numbers, *D&D* included so many game design ideas that it was extremely difficult for other designers to come up with anything new in the genre. Thus, RPG designers used three strategies for creating their own RPGs: simplification, combination, and specialization. I'm going to explain what each of those terms mean in the context of RPG history, but I want to point out now that it's the last of these strategies that *FFVII* follows. One mistake that I think many critics and players of today make about *FFVII* is assuming that its developers were trying to make a game like *Skyrim*, *Baldur's Gate*, or *Ultima* and simply failing. That's an easy mistake to make because the *Final Fantasy* series changed a lot between *FF1* and *FFVII*. Ultimately, the reason why *FFVII* lacks things like character classes, customization, and open-world gameplay is that it deliberately gives those things up in order to pursue something else.

In the Beginning: The Path to *D&D*

The RPG genre is built upon three essential design ideas: the simulated skill, level-ups, and orthogonal roles. These ideas didn't spontaneously appear in the RPG, but developed in a genre that preceded the RPG—the genre of wargames. The wargame with which most people are familiar is *Risk*. *Risk* features all the classic wargame ideas: players control zones on a map with miniature figurines. The figurines represent units in an army, and their strength depends in part on the roll of dice. Although *Risk* came out of the golden age of wargames, it is a simple example of a complicated genre. Although popular, it isn't quite as influential as most of the games we'll examine below, and despite being old by modern game standards, *Risk* is relatively recent in terms in the context of wargames. The wargame genre goes all the way back to the late 1700s, but the history of the genre first became specifically relevant to RPGs in the 1820s. The game in question is called *Kriegsspiel*, and it was the long term project of a father-and-son team of Prussian aristocrats.[1,2] Their goal was to improve the on-field tactical skills of Prussian army officers. Whether or not they succeeded is a matter for military historians, but their game is definitely the source of some important game design ideas. *Kriegsspiel* pits two military commanders against one another using small tokens that symbolize units within an army. The strength of those units depends heavily on the rolling of dice and factors like unit health, firing distance, differences in elevation, etc. A neutral umpire interprets the dice and other factors and tells the two combatants the result of their attempted actions.[3] Players of tabletop RPGs will immediately recognize what the neutral umpire eventually became: *the dungeon master (DM)*, a role which is tremendously important in the tabletop RPG.

The most important thing to recognize here is not the just the first documented existence of something like a DM, or the use dice to govern combat, but rather what they combine to accomplish. Taken all together, those things give us the simulated skill. A simulated skill is any skill that belongs entirely to a character in a game, rather than to the player who controls the character. In *Kriegsspiel*, the player doesn't have to do anything to attack except to declare to the umpire their intention, and then roll the dice.[4,5] The dice roll (simulating randomness), plus the umpire's interpretation of the circumstances of the attack (simulating battlefield conditions) account for all the execution.[6] Compare this to a game like basketball or *Super Mario Bros.* In those games, the player has to use manual dexterity and precise timing in order to perform crucial game functions. In a game like *Kriegsspiel* (or *FFVII* for that matter), all the dexterity, strength, and timing are simulated by numbers and rules. In RPGs, those stats are explicitly labeled "strength" or "dexterity." Wargames didn't really have that level of granularity until Gary Gygax and Jeff Perren came along, but *Kriegsspiel* still codified this idea by basing the strength of any given military unit on the current population of that unit.[7] In other words, the HP determines the damage. The execution is rudimentary, but it's still the same design idea upon which RPG skills depend to this day.

It would be almost 150 years before the other two pillars of the RPG evolved. The 1960s were the golden age of tabletop wargames, with their popularity growing markedly thanks to the formation of regional clubs, the publication of enthusiast periodicals, and the establishment of an annual conference where wargamers would gather to play.[8,9] The two creators of the RPG, Dave Arneson and Gary Gygax, were both avid players (as well as designers) of the genre, and they met for the first time at one of these conferences. The date was August 23, 1969 and the location was Horticultural Hall in Lake Geneva, Wisconsin, which the International Federation of Wargaming (of which Gygax was an officer) had rented out.[10] This conference was called the Geneva Convention—or GenCon for short—and tabletop gaming enthusiasts have attended it annually for nearly 50 years since. Dave Arneson was an undergraduate student studying history at the University of Minnesota and a central figure in a group of wargamers from the Twin Cities region. Gygax was older, a father of several children, and employed full-time as an insurance underwriter in Chicago.[11] Both of them were working on experimental wargames at the time, and it was the combination of these two experimental projects that would lead to the creation of *D&D*.

Gygax's most important game prior to *D&D* was *Chainmail*, a game he had been developing with his colleague Jeff Perren.[12] This game refined simulated skills and (almost accidentally) created the first character-level mechanic. *Chainmail* is a game that allows players to simulate the command of a relatively small number of medieval combatants. Although not especially original, *Chainmail's* rules are fairly easy and enjoyable to use, and allowed for low-population medieval combat.[13] (It was probably this last quality that motivated Arneson to borrow some of these rules for his own games—wargames of the 1960s tended to be enormous and enormously complicated.) The core *Chainmail* rules are historically important; many of the rules and concepts that first appeared in *Chainmail* would later appear as mechanics in *D&D*.[14] As I said earlier, however, these rules aren't historically novel; dozens of wargames had similar mechanics—it's just that *Chainmail's* ruleset was elegant and easy to use. The real innovation in *Chainmail* is in its appendix, the "Fantasy Supplement."

In the fantasy supplement, Gygax allowed players to use hero units that were significantly more powerful than their rank-and-file counterparts. Of course, these units had to obey the overall balance rules of the genre. In a typical wargame, each general is given a budget of points (e.g., 500 points) to allocate to different parts of his or her army. Footmen cost very little, perhaps one to five points to deploy. A heavily armed tower might cost 40 or more points to deploy because of its greater power.[15] The heroic units of *Chainmail's* fantasy supplement can cost more than 50 points to deploy because of their many tactical abilities. The really interesting thing is that the cost of a heroic unit can be scaled by "level." A wizard costs 100 points to deploy and has a large suite of skills like "Fireball" and "Magic Mist." The general can also deploy a lower-level hero, like a sorcerer—which Gygax calls a wizard minus 2. The sorcerer, although still much more powerful than a regular unit, is less powerful than a Wizard, but only costs 80 points to deploy.[17] In *Chainmail*, the point of reducing a hero's level is to reduce that hero's deployment cost, but hero level would soon serve a very different purpose when Dave Arneson got a hold of it.

Arneson's pet project at the time he met Gygax was called *Braunstein*, in which he developed the concept of orthogonal roles. *Braunstein* wasn't Arneson's original creation—that credit goes to David Wesely—but Arneson had continued development when the game's creator departed for military service.[18] *Braunstein* is notable for its introduction of orthogonal player roles. Up until this point, the players of a wargame generally occupied the same roles and had very similar victory conditions. Sometimes the starting conditions or victory conditions were slightly asymmetrical—but in almost every game, the player assumed the role of a military commander trying to pull off a narrow range military victories.[19] In *Braunstein*, two military commanders face off against one another, but there are also non-combatant player roles, like the chancellor of the university in the fictional town of *Braunstein* and the leader of the student union there. These roles are very different from the two generals; they have their own motivations, their own goals, and a non-military set of abilities.[20] The presence of non-military characters has an impact on the tactical considerations of the battlefield, but the more important (and less obvious) change brought on by non-military roles is

1. *Final Fantasy VII* and the History of RPGs

the ascendancy of playing a role in-character. The two military commanders in *Braunstein*, like the military commanders in any game, are driven by practical battlefield concerns. The orthogonal characters, like the student and the chancellor, are driven by their personal (narrative-driven) imperatives which are more dramatic than practical. The players who act as student, chancellor, and so on are all playing roles like actors might play them, but with significant game elements added to the drama.

Arneson combined the simulated skills of the traditional wargame, the orthogonal roles of *Braunstein*, and the proto-level mechanics of *Chainmail* to create the first game that could be called an RPG. The product of these ingredients was called *Blackmoor*. *Blackmoor* put these ideas to work in a format in which hero units could appear serially in a variety of qualitatively different adventures.[21] To make this possible, Arneson had to tweak each of the design ideas he inherited. The simple simulated skills of the wargame were not nearly granular enough to work for the variety of adventures that he had in mind. Using the same skill to swing swords, cast magic, and pick locks would be silly, and so Arneson and his group of fellow gamers created individual specialty skills like "strength," "courage," and "brains."[22] The neutral umpire role that was common to wargames wasn't sufficient for a linear format with more than two players. The umpire had to also play the role of author, nemesis, and referee, and thus the role of dungeon master was born. Orthogonal roles were translated directly and easily when they were combined with the different classes of hero from Gygax's Fantasy Supplement to allow players to play Warriors and Wizards. The defining idea, however, was the adaptation of hero levels. Instead of scaling a hero's level downwards to reduce his deployment cost, *Blackmoor* allows heroes to gain levels as they complete various activities.[23] This is a double simulation of skills, for a hero's level is both involved in calculating his current power and in tracking the ongoing acquisition of more power. This ongoing growth of character abilities is the glue which holds the serial quests of an RPG together and separates the genre from its wargame forebears.

The Titan in The Sand: The Overwhelming Legacy of *D&D*

The most famous product of Arneson and Gygax's experiments in game design is *D&D*, a game whose popularity has endured to this day. Although Arneson first put the form of the RPG together in *Blackmoor*, Gygax was quick to recognize its potential, and he massively expanded the game throughout the 1970s.[24–26] The company whose imprint *D&D* bore, Tactical Studies Rules, began to grow just as rapidly.[27] What was really remarkable about *D&D* was that it received so much development so quickly. In the late 1970s, the books which constituted *Advanced Dungeons & Dragons (AD&D)* came out, each of them rich in game design ideas. Below is a list of just some of the ideas found in those publications, which hopefully conveys the amount of development the RPG endured in those early years (Table 1.1).[28–30]

Table 1.1 Design Ideas First Appearing in *D&D*

Elemental affinity	Shared/pooled HP	Item enchantment	Knockdown
Damage vs type	Armor penetration	Item creation	Conjured equipment
Phased boss fights	Replenishing adds	Stealth/invisibility	Disable/destroy equips
Encounter rates	Fight past death	Gated levels	Stat soft-caps
Drop rates	Minimum range	Instant death attacks	Target segregation
Magic Resistance	Area of effect	Size-scaled interiors	Difficulty settings
Damage over time	Racial passives	Location-scaled time	Time-based abilities
Buffs	Stat thresholds	Casting reagents	Upkeep costs
Debuffs	Multi-class characters	Fast travel	Categorical item affixes
Armor classes	Resurrection penalties	Interrupts	Secondary professions
Stat substitution	Relative EXP	AC-independent block	Randomized inventories
EXP penalty	Channeled abilities	Spellcasting cooldowns	Debuff on crit
Terrain alteration	Spellcasting reagents	Enemy capture	Item identification
Healing over time	Item type highlighting	Damage floors/terrain	Hirelings
Back attacks	Thorns damage	Lighting levels	Fast travel

This table could easily be double or triple its current length, but that much documentation lies outside the purview of this book. The list is massive, however, and it only got longer as TSR released new material. There are two reasons why I show the list above. The first reason is that it can be astonishing to see how rapidly the designers of early RPGs created nearly all the mechanics which now define the genre. Then again, it shouldn't be astonishing. RPGs didn't come out of nowhere; they came out of an extremely rich tradition of wargames that stretched back more than a century. The point of that genre had always been to painstakingly simulate real historical battles, and numerous wargames had done just that, in different ways. *Dungeons & Dragons* operates by the same idea, but instead of historical battlefields, it simulates a Tolkienesque fantasy world. The speed at which the tabletop market pivoted from wargames to RPGs is remarkable, but it wasn't a fluke. This will be important later when we look at how—in the space of 10 years—*Final Fantasy* completely changed direction artistically and did something radical with the RPG. The second reason why I show this list is that it should be clear that by the time RPGs began to proliferate on computers and home consoles, they had already benefited from incredibly robust and wide-ranging rulesets. So vast were these rulesets that no digital form could ever implement them all.

(This is still true. No computer yet invented can hope to replicate the fecundity and flexibility of human imagination, but the restrictions in 1980 were even more limiting.) That limitation would cause RPG developers to employ three innovative strategies for creating their own distinct games.

The Necessary Simplification

With limited manpower and even more limited computer resources to draw upon, the early digital RPGs were mostly versions of *D&D*, or what I call simplifications. Games in the simplifications category simplify the *D&D* source material in order to make something like *D&D* possible on a computer—although they're not necessarily trying to recreate *D&D*. The first *Ultima* game (1981) is a good example of this phenomenon. Clocking in at about five to 10 hours, *Ultima* features most of the basic *D&D* design ideas, although it can't implement the massive freedom allowed by imaginative humans around a table. Moreover, although *Ultima* does the things *D&D* does, it rarely does them in quite the same way.[31] The level-up system and design of dungeons in the original *Ultima* are handled quite differently than their counterparts in mainline *D&D* Campaigns. With one exception—a poorly integrated and brief shooter section—*Ultima* only does things that were already hallmarks of *D&D*. This is the nature of simplifications; games of this type inherit the scope of *D&D*, but not all its methods. Changing the methods changes the feel of the game significantly, but it doesn't constitute an original invention. Other games which fall into this category are *Wizardry* (1980), *The Bard's Tale* (1985), *Might and Magic* (1986), and *Baldur's Gate* (1998)—or many of the sequels in those series. Each successive game in those series moved closer to the kind of scope a great *D&D* campaign would have because that was always the ultimate goal of the simplification strategy. I'm sure that some tabletop enthusiasts have noticed that I haven't mentioned any of the other major pen-and-paper RPGs that influenced videogame designers, like *Runequest, Traveler,* or *GURPS*. In my view, none of those games expand the scope of the RPG form in a way that *D&D* did not do first. Indeed, most of the *D&D* editions to come out after 1989 didn't expand the scope either, although they and their competitors still have plenty of value. Starting with *AD&D*, one of the most important tasks for designers at TSR was to revise the massive array of game design ideas which came from Gygax, who produced great concepts but often used bizarre implementations. The efforts of Gygax's successors were crucial because execution is at least as important—or perhaps more important—as the concepts they execute. Mediocre concepts can make for fun games when implemented particularly well; great concepts implemented poorly rarely succeed.

RPG Plus X

Simplification is the easiest strategy to identify because it followed *D&D* so immediately and in such a clear way. Simplification is not, however, the most popular strategy for escaping the encircling influence of *D&D*. The most popular strategy is combination. Combination is simply the practice of combining RPGs with another genre. The practice of combining two genres in a videogame is a very historically important one that led to an entire school of game design. (You can read much more about this history in the *Reverse Designs* of *Super Mario World* and *Half-Life*.) Role-playing games are no exception to this trend. The most famous product of the union of native-videogame genres with RPG design ideas is the action-RPG. One of the big successes of the action RPG is the inroads it made into the console market in games like *Secret of Mana* (1993) or *A Link to the Past* (1991).

Although action RPGs employ many RPG ideas that first appeared in traditional RPGs, they also feature a huge variety of fresh action game ideas. Indeed, the proliferation of action game ideas throughout the 1980s and 1990s ensured that action RPG designers never had to worry about being different from *D&D*. Action game tropes, injected into an RPG mold, made for games that seemed fresh and distinct. Certainly, real-time (or at least limited-time) play was a house rule in plenty of otherwise traditional *D&D* campaigns, but none of those games could have offered the kind of dexterity/speed challenges that a console game could.

The action RPG was one of the first fruits of the marriage of RPGs and extant videogame genres, but it is hardly the only one; RPG ideas have infiltrated all manner of games. For example, the FPS/RPG hybrid is a fairly old one, but it has come to spectacular prominence since 2008 in games like *Deus Ex: Human Revolution* (2011) and the three newest entries in the *Fallout* Series. The combinations are apparently endless, and sometimes quite surprising. *ActRaiser* (1990) combines a somewhat standard action RPG with a city-building overworld game. This is a combination that would eventually also appear (although in a very different style) in *Minecraft* (2011). Although RPG elements are nearly ubiquitous in contemporary game design, not every genre uses them liberally. The one genre (aside from RPGs themselves) that uses lots of RPG elements (and uses them well) is the tower defense genre. Although there isn't enough space to cover them all in this book, two great examples are *Gemcraft: Labyrinth* (2011) and *Defender's Quest* (2012), which execute incredibly deep RPG mechanics in a tower defense framework.

A Small Slice of a Genre

Designers who did not want to combine their RPG with something else, and did not attempt to recreate the whole of *D&D* employed the last strategy, which I call specialization. If *D&D* was too massive to recreate, but too artistically complete to avoid entirely, designers had one other option: pick a part of the *D&D* formula and embellish it. The best way to explain this is by using an early example. The 1980 game *Rogue* uses all of the essential RPG mechanics that were codified in *D&D*, but it focuses entirely on dungeon exploration. There is no plot. There are minimal NPCs (shopkeepers travelling through the dungeon at random), but there are no towns, no charisma checks—there is only dungeon-crawling. By stripping away everything that isn't a dungeon, *Rogue* is able to get players in and out of combat very quickly. Whereas dying in a typical *D&D* campaign can slow the game down as players pursue ways of replacing or resurrecting their party members, *Rogue* doesn't even allow for any of that. After death, the player is immediately back in a dungeon, fighting, disarming traps, and looting treasure. Simplification-type games drop parts of the *D&D* scope because they can't fit them in—it's a practical decision. Specialization-type games, on the other hand, drop parts of the *D&D* scope in order to deliberately reduce scope and embellish a smaller set of design ideas—it's an artistic decision.

An entire subgenre sprang from what *Rogue* did first. The roguelike genre, although it has changed over the years, is more popular now than ever before. *Nethack, Diablo, FTL*, and *The Binding of Isaac* are just a few of the most well-known titles in that burgeoning subgenre. *Final Fantasies VI* and *VII* are some of the first non-roguelike games that employed the strategy of specialization to great success. Both games would focus primarily on the storytelling and/or world-building aspects of the RPG: rich characterization, fantastic but persuasive settings, and thoughtful, meaningful quests. One of the really interesting things about this change is that it happened to a series that started as a simplification. Another interesting turn is that at the same point where the *Final Fantasy* series was entering its most idiosyncratic form, other RPGs started to appear that employed the same strategy in different ways. We'll reflect on that after we see how *Final Fantasy* went from simplification to specialization across its first seven titles.

Final Fantasy as a Series of Increasingly Interesting Protagonists

One of the widespread features of a simplification-type game is a blank or minimalist protagonist. This is an unimpressive fact for me to unveil, but I think that the bland protagonist is actually a great barometer for the type of RPG a given game wants to be. In a *D&D* campaign, the protagonist is a fluid expression of the player's imagination and can make whatever choices the player and DM agree are possible. This freedom of action and characterization were the first casualties of the transition from tabletop to digital formats. No computer can hope to recreate the human imagination, and so no player-character can embody the choices and personality traits that its player would enjoy in a tabletop setting. The simplified design idea which many games still use in place of a fully-acted character is a minimalist protagonist who primarily makes practical choices. The heroes of *Ultima* and *Wizardry* have essentially nothing in the way of defined personality. There are plenty of decisions for the protagonist/player to make, but most of them have to do with practical problems: which query will get the innkeeper to dispense a quest? Which query will get secret information out of the roadside traveler? Do I kill this creature or spare its life? These decisions tend to be performed as shrewd calculations rather than as expressions of an imaginary person with consistent traits and a dramatic arc. This doesn't mean that these games lack characterization entirely. The later *Ultima* games are famous for the depth and complex interactivity of their NPCs, but the simplification style did force RPG designers to treat their protagonists in a reductive way to preserve some sense of the original tabletop freedom. The *Final Fantasy* series features bland and/or blank protagonists for its first five games as well. Retrospectively, *FF* titles are well known for the variety of vibrant and memorable characters they have—and that was true as far back as *FFIV*—but the protagonists of those early *FF* games were thin. In the first three games, they were effectively silent except for quest-based keywords. It wasn't until *FFIV* and *FFV* that protagonists started to have real dialogue, and even then they didn't have anything particularly personal to say.

Cecil and Bartz/Butz have feelings distinct from the players that control them. Yet, most of what they say and feel is unfailingly (and blandly) heroic. Cecil and Bartz mostly want and feel things that will push the quest forward. Moreover, these two designated protagonists are the least interesting members of their respective parties from a characterization standpoint. Really, all of the early *FF* protagonists are necessary and unsurprising because the first five titles in the *Final Fantasy* series fall into the simplification type of RPG. Yes, there are some important divergences in these games from the *D&D* source materials. *Final Fantasy* titles (like most Japanese RPGs) allow the player to gain vastly more levels in a single campaign than a Western RPG does, although each level was less meaningful to balance those gains. Also like many other Japanese RPGs, critical hits and critical failures are a much less important part of the game. Job classes and party composition are still paramount, and protagonists are still mostly-blank canvases onto which the player can project their own ideas.

The first really radical *FF* title is *FFVI*. Critics have long held that *FFIV* was where the series started to distinguish itself and become the series that we know today. In terms of plots, settings and art concepts, I think that might be true. The journey that *FFIV* takes the player on is pretty wild, and includes an accelerated-time pocket dimension, the hollow underside of an entire world, and a trip to the moon. More importantly in *FFIV*, a ton of characters move in and out of the party, which would end up being a very *Final Fantasy* thing to do. The thing that prevents *FFIV* from being radical is party composition. Every character in *FFIV* has a job class with strengths and weaknesses. Party composition and character roles are an important tactical part of the game, but with all those characters coming and going, the party is kind of a mess until it stabilizes (in a totally orthodox configuration) late in the game. Party composition alone makes some dungeons and bosses inappropriately hard or easy for the point of the game in which they appear. *Final Fantasy VI* is able to maintain a large roster of characters without any practical problems by diminishing the importance of character classes. There are 14 characters to play in *FFVI*, and any four of them are totally viable as a main party. The two lower-level design ideas that make this possible are greatly revised magic mechanics and the availability of powerful armor for any class. Because of the way the magic damage formula works in *FFVI*, any character can be turned into a serviceable mage—in addition to being an engineer, samurai, or monk.

What's more, the characters who are mages can equip allegedly "light" armor which is statistically equal to or even better than some of the best "heavy" armor in the game. This abandonment of the tactical differences between character classes is the first real move by *Final Fantasy* toward becoming a specialization-type game instead of a traditional simplification.

The diminution of character classes is a profound artistic decision and a huge departure from the RPG heritage, but it allows the *Final Fantasy* games of the mid-and late-1990s to do something artistically bold. More than 150 years of tactical heritage were cut out of *FFVI* in a single decision, but look what it allows the game to do: *FFVI* has no clear protagonist. One can argue Terra is the "main" character, but she's far from being the most talkative character in the game.[32]

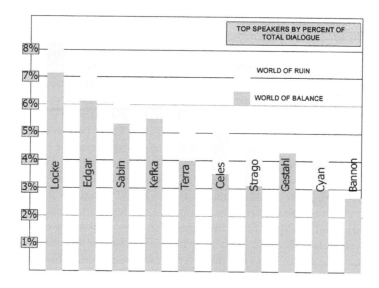

TOP SPEAKERS BY PERCENT OF TOTAL DIALOGUE

WORLD OF RUIN

WORLD OF BALANCE

Locke · Edgar · Sabin · Kefka · Terra · Celes · Strago · Gestahl · Cyan · Bannon

Terra is very important to *FFVI*, but the plot of the second half does not revolve around her. Indeed, it's possible to beat the game without her. This is because when the World of Ruin begins, Terra is off on her own deeply personal quest.

Irrespective of the player's wishes, Terra finds her own meaning by becoming the guardian of the Mobliz orphans. Terra wants to love and be loved by a group of minor characters the player may not care much about. Even if she is the protagonist, her struggle is not just the bland, uniform destiny of a world-saving hero; it's much more human in scale and idiosyncratic in nature. The same is true for most of the characters of *FFVI*—they all find personal reasons to continue their fight against a world that seems hopeless.

The player isn't given the traditional RPG freedoms, choices, and tactical puzzles to solve, but in place of those things, the player gets to explore a thoughtfully-imagined world with a group of people they can really care about. That's exactly the kind of artistic trade-off that typifies a specialization-type game.

All of the trends that make *FFVI* a radical game exist in *FFVII* to an even greater degree. The diminution of character classes is the most obvious trend. In *FFVI*, characters have classes, but the differences between those classes are less important than in other RPGs. In *FFVII*, there is only one character that has a clear job class: Aeris. Aeris is obviously a mage; she is the only character that starts in the back row. She has significantly lower attack and defense stats, but compensates for these with well-above-average magic stats. Other characters have slight strengths and weaknesses, but none of them have defined roles. Except for Aeris, everyone is a jack-of-all-trades. Accordingly, it's even easier for the player to put the party together for plot-and-character reasons. Every party member has unique dialogue for almost every scene in the game, and that dialogue is always written in-character. If *FFVII* is dropping one part of the RPG formula to embellish another in the manner of a specialization, it seems that the designers are still interested (as they were in *FFVI*) in embellishing characterization and storytelling at the expense of tactical composition. To be fair, all RPG designers want their players to care about the characters in their games, but in *FFVII* that "care" means something different. Tabletop players care about their own characters because those characters are the projections of their own imaginations. They care about the other party members because those party members are the creations of their real-life friends, and/or because those party members are tactically necessary. Players care about the characters in *FFVII* because they are compellingly written.

If any of the above sounds like an attempt to persuade you to like *FFVII*, let me clarify that it is not. As I said in the introduction, the purpose of this book is not to debate personal preferences, but rather to show that people who like *FFVII* and people who don't have both missed seeing *FFVII* for all that it is. One thing I think many people have missed about the game is the almost absurdly radical way it characterizes its protagonist. *Final Fantasy VI* had shown that the console RPG audience was perfectly willing to exchange the customizable protagonist and character classes of traditional RPGs for well-drawn, sympathetic characters and a compelling plot. In *FFVII*, the designers take things further. Like the many characters of *FFVI*, Cloud Strife is not a mostly-blank canvas but fully-realized character with his own feelings, mannerisms and opinions. When he's not thinking about Sephiroth, he has a certain laid-back folksiness to him.

This is a pretty far cry from the typical card-carrying hero that occupies other RPGs from this era. Most of the player-characters in *FFVII* are drawn with the same level of care, but Cloud is the protagonist and he has a special extra flourish. He is also an unreliable narrator, which is common enough in other forms of narrative, but rare in videogames.

The original Western audience of *FFVII* also grew up in the era of *Fight Club*, *American Psycho*, and *Memento*—popular movies that feature various kinds of unreliable narrators. None of those films offer the kind of connection to their protagonists that *FFVII* does, however. I don't mean that the protagonists of those films aren't well drawn, but rather that the player of *FFVII* has to rely on Cloud in a way that the viewer of a film does not. When the player wants to explore a town or dungeon, they use Cloud's body to do it. When they want to talk to an NPC,

1. *Final Fantasy VII* and the History of RPGs

Cloud is their representative. If he falls in battle, the party is in serious trouble. It doesn't matter that he's not a typical vessel for player projections—there's still a strong association between the player and Cloud. That association is idiosyncratic feature of both videogames and RPGs in general. When the player finds out that the character they rely on for all of these functions isn't actually who he says he is, it is a deeply unnerving moment. It's almost as if the player's *arm* has been lying to him or her. Not every player is going to appreciate the effect, obviously, but that doesn't make it any less radical. Amnesia and deceit are common enough tropes in RPGs, but as far as I have been able to tell, no RPG has ever deliberately betrayed the connection between protagonist and player like *FFVII* does. It's a bold, subversive artistic maneuver that—like it or not—sets *FFVII* apart.

The Age of Specializations

Before moving on to Chapter 2, I want to take a very brief look at *FFVII's* historical context from a few other perspectives. At the same time that *FFVII* was eliminating character classes and tactical party composition to make room for more plot and characterization, a different Japanese RPG was doing almost the exact opposite. The original *Pokémon* titles (1996) are essentially entirely about character classes and party composition. To that end, the game diminishes almost all the other parts of the RPG form. The expurgation is incredibly thorough:

- There is very little plot
- There are relatively few NPCs
- There is almost no characterization of anyone whatsoever
- There is very little non-linear exploration
- There are no choices except choosing between Pokémon
- There is almost nothing to do except fight

All those hundreds of Pokémon constitute an extremely elaborate job-class system. The choice between Staryu and Kingler is a much finer one than the choice between warrior and rogue (or even warrior and paladin), but the type of choice is the same. *Pokémon* is a specialization that hardly bothers with anything except building the perfect team composition. Whether or not they actually enjoy playing the games, most critics recognize that *Pokémon* is one of the most brilliant RPGs of all time. What's strange is that nobody has ever faulted *Pokémon* for being different from traditional Western RPGs. In fact, very few people even identify Pokémon as being a part of the nebulous JRPG category. *Pokémon* and *FFVII* are the results of the same artistic strategy—specialization. In their own contexts, they're both well executed (the rest of this book will argue the case for *FFVII's* execution), but I think that the best thing we can do, as critics and fans, is to accept that some games can be artistically successful even if we don't like them. *Final Fantasy VII* doesn't fail to be a big, open, Western RPG; it was never trying to be like that in the first place.

The other perspective we can use to examine *FFVII* (and *Pokémon* for that matter) is seeing if the changes they make to the RPG have any basis in the RPG tradition and become something else entirely. That is, does *FFVII's* intense specialization strip away the essence of the RPG? This is where the history is really useful because we know exactly how the RPG came about. If you look at RPGs as an extension of wargames, then you could say that *FFVII* is no longer a part of that continuum. By eliminating essentially all of the RPG's tactical heritage, *FFVII* stops being an RPG and becomes something else—an adventure game or an interactive movie that dabbles in RPG stats. Yet, wargames existed for more than 150 years before RPGs emerged. Then, almost as though a switch had flipped, RPGs exploded in popularity and displaced wargames in the tabletop space. This could not have happened if it weren't for the third and final pillar of RPG design: orthogonal roles. The simulated skills that came from wargames are the bones of the RPG—they give the genre structure. The heart and soul of the RPG, that which makes the genre truly distinct, is the characters that populate it. These characters came about through the use of assigned, orthogonal roles. Party members, villains, and other assorted NPCs are what make RPG worlds persuasive. In an interview he did late in his life, Gary Gygax spoke about his distaste for the kind of quest

> [T]hat has little more in it than seek and destroy missions, vacuous effort where the participants fight and kill some monster so as to gain more power and thus be able to look for yet more potent opponents in a spiral that leads nowhere save eventual boredom. So pure hack and slash play is anathema to me, too.[33]

I think this quote shows that the creation of persuasive worlds and characters was always at the center of the RPG. *Final Fantasy VII* is, therefore, true to the essence of RPGs, even if its style is deeply divisive.

1. *Final Fantasy VII* and the History of RPGs

2

Narrative and Design

Because the narrative aspects of a JRPG are a feature of design as much as anything else in the game, we have to study them with an eye toward the practical necessities of design. With everything we've seen about *FFVII's* place in the history of RPGs, we know that the story was of central importance to the design of this particular game as much as any JRPG ever. Now, I have said before, and I will repeat here again, that I will not make a defense of the literary qualities of *FFVII*. To my knowledge, nobody has ever praised the prosody of *FFVII* in English or in the original Japanese. The inconsistent translation for which it is famous certainly did not help. Other assessments about the story's literariness are a matter of taste and I won't debate them. I think, however, that there are some structural ideas from which we can glean quite a bit of useful RPG design knowledge. When I say "structural," I'm referring to two concrete ideas: the character design and the measurable way in which the story is told, line by line. Character design is something as old as the RPG format; players and dungeon masters have had to design characters for their campaigns since the first edition of *D&D*. *Final Fantasy VII's* characters are, as we'll see, the product of a well-established game design process. That is, the important people in *FFVII* are designed in the same way a level designer might generate the contents of a platformer. The other way in which we can analyze the structure of *FFVII's* storytelling (in the second half of this chapter) is by seeing how the story is delivered on a line-by-line basis. It's not the nuances in the language we're interested in here, but rather a statistical analysis of how story and dialogue are meted out over the entire course of the game. As a meaningful point of comparison, we'll see how *FFVII's* statistical profile measures up to a novel of similar length (and similar themes), F. Scott Fitzgerald's *The Great Gatsby*.

Do the Designers Really Want to Say Something Meaningful?

Before talking about the narrative of *FFVII*, I want to show that it is a subject that has not received nearly enough attention. Earlier, I argued that the game is about survivors—people who have outlived the worlds that defined them. Below, I am going to show how this is true for each character, but I realize how easy it would be to believe that I have cherry-picked all my evidence and that most of the game is inconsistent with my thesis. After all, this game is nearly 20 years old at the time of this writing and—as far as I know—nobody has ever made this claim before. To show how pervasive this theme actually is, I want to give a few examples from the setting of the game. During the escape from the first reactor, the party has a conversation about the history and geography of Midgar.

2. Narrative and Design

It's easy to overlook that the game is already communicating its central theme through the setting. *Final Fantasy VII* is a game about people who have outlived the world that once defined them. Midgar is the embodiment of this. It is a new city built over an old city—a new world order literally burying the past. Yet, the buried people of the slums, for the most part, cannot move on from the place that gave them their identities. In that regard, they're quite a lot like the player characters. The key difference, as we'll see shortly, is that the connection the player characters have to the past motivates them to action.

Although it's easy to miss because it happens mostly as passing NPC chatter, this idea of people who have lost their identity is reiterated in many of the towns across the world of *FFVII*. Kalm, Junon, Corel, Rocket Town, and Wutai all used to be something far different than they are now.

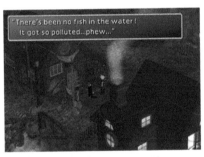

In every case, the original inhabitants of the town have lost what defined them, and in some cases, nothing has really replaced what was lost. Although a few of the residents of these towns have found ways to live in their new world, most of them seem lost now that their identities are irrelevant to the world that Shinra has created.

Another thing most people have overlooked as a vehicle for the theme is the limit break system. These days, critics put special emphasis on consonance between narrative and mechanics. I don't intend to make that issue a big part of my examination of *FFVII*, but the limit break is one place where we can see such a consonance. The limit break system rewards the player for keeping the characters alive through large amounts of damage.

For every attack the player characters survive, the limit meter fills; the bigger the attack, the greater the gain—but if the player dies, the limit meter empties. In other words, the limit break is a reward for surviving, not a reward for taking damage. This is a reflection of the general theme of survivorship in the game. It isn't a particularly insightful example of the theme: limit breaks are acts of violent rage. By the end of the game, the characters in *FFVII* all transcend that rage. Despite this inelegance, the limit break system does reflect the main theme of the game. What's more, a number of player limit breaks (which need to be unlocked by items) are found in meaningful locations that tie the characters to their pasts. A widow in Corel gives Barret his ultimate limit break, Lucrecia gives Vincent his, a letter from Zangan contains Tifa's limit break, and a reward from Godo gives Yuffie hers. Not every limit break in the game is so thematically located, but I think it's meaningful that a few of them are. In the section below, we'll see how survivorship and an empowering connection to the past are two parts of a three-part checklist that defines the way that the characters were created in accordance with the game's main theme.

Characters and the Ludic Method That Made Them

The creation of characters is, and always has been, a facet of game design. In Chapter 1, I explained how Dave Arneson's principal contribution to the RPG was the roles that characters played. From his experiences modifying and refereeing Braunstein, he understood that the RPG would depend heavily upon the player's investment into the character they role-play. This idea carried right over into computer and console RPGs. A well-designed role/character gives its player an overarching reason to push through dungeons and battles. Not everyone needs a reason to go questing; some players will do dungeons for the sake of doing dungeons. For the audience that Arneson originally imagined, characters and their motivations were just as much a part of the minute-by-minute gameplay as dice-rolls and stat tables. Any examination of *FFVII* as a work of art must take into account the design of characters as an essential game design task. From a purely practical perspective, consider how well the motivations of the characters work to drive the plot. *Final Fantasy VII* has 31 quests, but none of them consist of collecting eight snow-hare tails, killing 12 giant dragonflies, or curing four cursed treants. Every quest is relevant to the plot, and it's always fairly obvious why the characters are pursuing it. If that isn't enough, each of the party members and most of the villains embody the theme of the game (outliving a world that gave them their identity) in a different way. Indeed, the way that the characters were designed is actually idiosyncratic to games. Because they were game designers, the *FFVII* team implemented the idea of survivors in an iterative way. To illustrate what I mean by this, I'm going to cite a completely different type of game. One of my favorite levels in *Super Mario World* is Chocolate Fortress. In the second half of that level, there's a long section that is made up of just three elements: a Thwomp, a Thwimp, and a pit.

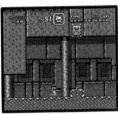
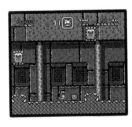
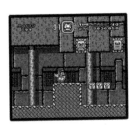
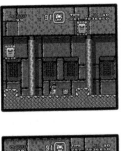
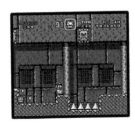
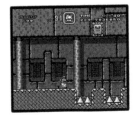

To keep the level interesting and fill it out with content, the designers do all manner of different things with those three elements. They combine them in every possible way, add and subtract things, and even change the shape of the level, but they never add a fourth element. The *FFVII* team practices the same kind of innovative iteration, except they do it with character design. In place of a barrel and a bee, the *FFVII* team has three ideas, what I call the "survivor's trio," which apply to nearly every character and the main villains. With one important exception, all the main characters:

1. Have lost the world that defined them
2. Have had near-death experiences
3. Have someone or something that connects them to the past and motivates them in their quest

For some characters this is obvious and for others it is subtle, but for each main character, we'll see how the designers manage to fulfill these three characteristics in different (and very game-like) ways. I've already talked about Barret enough, but I do want to point out that he has all three of these criteria. He lost the world that defined him (Corel), he had a near-death experience (having his arm shot off), and he has someone in his life that connects him to his past and motivates him in his quest (Marlene). All but one of the characters have these three elements somehow worked into their design.

Protagonists

Besides Barret, Tifa has the most typical story of a near-death experience and the loss of a world she belonged to, but the person who connects her to the past is anything but typical. Tifa was nearly killed by Sephiroth during his rampage in Nibelheim. Her world was destroyed, her friends and loved ones murdered, and if Zangan's letter hidden in her piano is true, she survived against long odds. Those two details are quite similar to Barret's experience, but the contrast between Marlene and Cloud—who are Barret and Tifa's respective connections to the past—is stark. Marlene represents all the memories Barret has of Corel, and all his hopes for a future in a world free from the control of Shinra Inc. Tifa's connection to her past is different. Cloud represents the only living connection to her previous world, but their relationship is nothing like that of Barret and Marlene. Although the player only learns of Cloud's psychosis late in the game, Tifa knows about it the whole time. Cloud is unstable, a compulsive liar, and in possession of a set of deadly skills and weapons. His behavior and motivations are suspect and at key moments, he even appears to be under the control of the very same person who murdered her father. Critics of *FFVII* have often made the mistake of thinking Tifa longs for Cloud romantically. She may have these feelings at the end of the game, but it's not clear that this is the case in the middle of it.

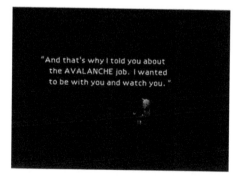

2. Narrative and Design

Tifa wants to believe that some part of her past still lives—that she shares her identity and the destruction of it—with someone else. She is so desperate to have this that she will endure all of Cloud's eerie behavior, and will even help him to maintain an illusion she knows isn't true.

Although she clearly cares about Cloud, Tifa's underlying reason for denying her suspicions is a selfish desire for a connection to her past, not a patient acceptance of Cloud's troubles. She's not even sure that the person before her is Cloud, but she'll take whatever connection she can get. There's so much humanity in that contradiction, though. Tifa's selfishness—her need to be connected to the past through Cloud—ends up doing her as much harm as good.

Although almost every party member adheres to the formula of loss of identity, near-death experience, and a motivating connection to the past through a single person or thing, it's not always as clear as it is with Tifa and Barret. Such is the case with Cid. Although we hear very little of it, Cid belonged to a world that ceased to be when the war between Wutai and Midgar ended.

The NPC chatter in Rocket Town makes it clear that Cid was a very important figure in the Shinra Air Force, and at the end of the war he was going to finish his career by going into space. Cid aborts the launch to save Shera's life, and the space program is subsequently defunded as Shinra switches from being a weapons manufacturer to be a utility company. Cid has nothing to fall back on now that the war is over, and the party finds him brooding over his lost ambition. In Cid's case, it's not entirely clear whether the thing that ties him to his past is Shera or the rocket itself. On the one hand, he certainly blames Shera and relives his frustration every time he sees her. On the other hand, the party encounters Cid in the rocket—where he spends most of days. He obviously hasn't moved on, even while a town has sprung up around the infrastructure left by the launch site. Cid's near-death experience, too, is easy to miss. The malfunctioning tank that Shera was working on during the original launch really does explode, and very well might have killed Cid the first time he tried to get into outer space. Just because Cid wasn't aware of how close he was to death doesn't mean he didn't narrowly miss a cruel fate. It's easy to see Cid as a throw-in character because he isn't wracked with guilt, anguish, or grief. While Cid's brash reaction to the loss of his identity is different from most of the other characters, he still fits the same pattern as the rest of the party.

Vincent is in a similar situation to Cid in that he was discarded by Shinra, Inc. A former Turk (secret police), he didn't necessarily lose a world that gave him his identity, he lost his very humanity when Hojo experimented on him. One might say that Vincent didn't have a near-death experience as much as he had an undeath experience. His connection to the past, meanwhile, is a bit more remote than those of other characters, but it fits the pattern well. The party does eventually encounter Lucrecia, who is Sephiroth's human mother. Although she appears in only one scene, she nevertheless fulfils the criterion of connecting Vincent to the past and motivating him in his ongoing quest. Indeed, she does a better job of bringing back the past than most of the minor characters in the game. The flashback in Lucrecia's cavern is the only time the player gets any explanation of Sephiroth's actual parentage or any background on what Shinra was like before and during the war. Despite the brevity of her appearance, Lucrecia definitely does accomplish for Vincent what Marlene, Cloud, and the rocket/Shera do for their respective characters.

Red XIII's adherence to the survivor's trio seems, at first glance, more tenuous than it really is. Red XIII did have a near-death experience, but we never see it play out on screen. Red XIII's near-death experience was during the battle between his people and the tribe of the Gi. Although it isn't clear what ultimately happened after Seto made his last stand, Red XIII is the only member of his race the player ever meets, so obviously his escape from death was fairly narrow, as the aftermath of the event claimed every other member of his tribe. Like Aeris, Red XIII is the last of his kind, or at least the last of his kind that anyone knows about. His survivorship in a world to which he doesn't belong is about as literal as it gets. His connection to the past is equally obvious and literal. One of Bugenhagen's primary roles in the game is as a historian of the planet and of Cosmo Canyon. Because of his personal affection for Red XIII, Bugenhagen shows him the true story of his past and directs him explicitly to continue his quest. That's about as straightforward an implementation of those two principles as exists in any character, even if we only hear about most of these events secondhand.

If any party character actually lacks one of the three elements in particular, it's Yuffie. There's no clear near-death experience in her past. Her defeat by the party might count as one, but she seems perfectly fine afterwards, so it's not a very good example. Like Red XIII, she may have been greatly endangered in a past we only hear about when Wutai was subdued. According to Elmyra's story about Aeris's origin, the war in Wutai was still producing casualties when Yuffie would have been a child, but this is admittedly vague. Her connection to the past and survival in a world where she doesn't belong are both fairly clear, however. Wutai itself is the thing that connects her to her past.

Yuffie wishes to regain Wutai's lost warrior tradition through a kind of bastardized vision of the ninja identity. Moreover, it's not entirely clear that Yuffie is old enough to really remember what Wutai and its people were like before the war. But even if she's not correct, Yuffie is still connected to and motivated by that past in the same way that the rest of the characters are.

Like the straight man in a comedy act, or the control in a scientific study, Cait Sith provides contrast. He doesn't have any of the survivor's trio, but this is a deliberate choice that highlights what the other characters have in common. I do not like to separate Cait Sith from the character who controls him, Reeve. Although Reeve speaks much differently in his own persona than he does when operating his fortune-telling dummy, his interests and motivations are not clearly different when he is "in character." Reeve has a genuine interest in the party, as he explains.

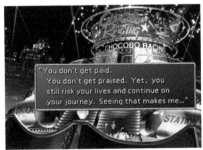

Reeve does not start out a survivor. Reeve starts the game in a context that not only defines him, but gives him power. From the moment that President Shinra drops the Sector Seven plate, however, Reeve's power is progressively eroded. By the end of the game, he has been removed from his position, and then Shinra itself collapses. Although Reeve doesn't have a near-death experience (one of Cait Sith's bodies dies, if that counts) or an obvious connection to a past that motivates him, he does end up in the same condition as the rest of the party: he has outlived the context (Shinra, Inc.) that gave him his identity.

Aeris clearly exhibits the survivor's trio, but with an important variation. Obviously, she is the last of the Cetra, and she has therefore outlived the world they inhabited. She spends much of her screen time trying to reconnect to that past with increasing (although tragic) success. Equally obvious is her connection to the past: the Holy Materia that she received from her mother. The variation is in her near-death experience—she doesn't actually survive it. The plot demands Aeris's death, but I think many critics have overlooked the symbolic communication embedded in that death. Aeris is the only character with a job class, even though it isn't explicitly stated. She's physically weak and has a low defense. All of her limit breaks are support-based. She is the only character in the game that is in the back row by default. The *FFVII* designers, many of whom were veterans of the earlier games in the series, were entirely aware of the diminution of job classes in *FFVI* and *FFVII*. Aeris's death is, in part, a commentary on that. In the plot, Aeris has to die to activate the Holy Materia. To make a game as dependent on plot and characterization as *FFVII*, character classes have to die. The mixing of drama and symbolic communication is little appreciated because people typically don't expect it from videogames of the 90s. Nevertheless, it's in there.

Cloud and His Many Personas

Cloud is the character most difficult to talk about, not because he doesn't fit the formula (he does), but rather because it's easy to miss all the avant-garde things the designers do with him. The way in which Cloud deals with outliving his context serves as a major basis for the plot. Cloud suffered exactly what Tifa suffered: the loss of a hometown, the death of a parent, and horrific sword wounds, but his delusions stem from the added burden of shame. Cloud was so unable to deal with his losses, his failure to join SOLDIER, and his failure to protect his hometown and his loved ones that he has to steal someone else's identity in order to keep living. By becoming a version of Zack, Cloud steals an identity to replace the one he lost. (Although, as we'll see, this wasn't the first identity he tried to assume.) Cloud's dedication to this facade is, on its face, absurd. He must have known that Tifa would see through his version of the events in Nibelheim, and yet he can't even admit this to himself while he's telling the story. Cloud lacks the personal force and organizational power to insist upon this false persona the way a politician or celebrity might do, so it's hard to understand his dedication to the charade. Yet his dedication is bizarrely intense. When Sephiroth punctures his assumed persona as an ex-SOLDIER, Cloud accepts an identity as a clone rather than admit (to himself and everyone else) who he really is.

Cloud helplessly begs Hojo to give him a third identity, a third context to give his being meaning. What really makes this a pathetic move (in all senses of the word) is how diminutive it is. Cloud is begging for a number—begging to be labeled as a nameless science project, a mere derivative thing. He's willing to accept Sephiroth and Hojo's denigration—he's even eager for it! Compared to that level of agonizing vulnerability, his charade of pretending to be Zack seems sane.

Cloud's connection to the past is definitely the most complex aspect of his survivor's trio, but it also helps to explain why he is the way he is. His connection to the past isn't Tifa, or Nibelhim, or even Zack; Cloud's connection to the past is Sephiroth. Earlier, I said that when *FFVII* appears to be about revenge, it is really a deconstruction of a revenge story. Too often, critics use the term deconstruction only to mean that a work of art does the opposite of what an audience expects. In *FFVII*, and in the particular case of Cloud, it means something a little less polar. Instead of reversing expectations, the *FFVII* team carefully unpacks Cloud's desire to defeat Sephiroth, and through this process they reveal Cloud's personality more deeply. Cloud explicitly says at more than one point that he wants to settle the score with Sephiroth, but for all his focus on fighting Sephiroth, Cloud isn't overly confrontational with him when the two of them are face to face.

Cloud doesn't gloat, he doesn't taunt Sephiroth, and he doesn't scream or curse at him, even when they're one-on-one. The closest thing to actual venom Cloud ever manages is when he tells Sephiroth to "Shut up" at the water altar in the Forgotten City. If we try to understand Cloud's overarching goal in terms other than sadistic glee, it makes more sense. When Cloud tells the rest of the party that they need to find their own motivation for the last battle, he explains his own motivation in personal terms.

This would be an odd way to say "I need to make Sephiroth feel the pain that I felt." That's what one might expect from a straightforward revenge story, but that's not what we see. It's also not the case that Cloud is merely putting on a tough-guy façade and speaking only rarely. As we'll see in Chapter 3, Cloud speaks way more words than any other character in the game. The whole point of Cloud's revelation in the Lifestream is that he no longer has to pretend to be a disinterested mercenary. Instead of a mere desire to kill or cause harm, Cloud needs to defeat Sephiroth in order to be able to live as himself.

To understand what it means for Cloud to really be himself, we have to zoom out (so to speak) and look at Cloud's entire life, with particular attention to the subtle symmetry between him and Sephiroth. During the catastrophe at Nibelheim, Cloud stabs Sephiroth, gravely wounding him. Sephiroth returns the favor shortly thereafter. Cloud throws Sephiroth into the Lifestream, and during his journey through it, Sephiroth learns his true identity as a descendent of Jenova. Five years later, after the events in the Whirlwind Maze, Sephiroth dumps Cloud into the Lifestream. With a little help from Tifa, Cloud discovers his true identity there, too.

2. Narrative and Design

Another very important thing is revealed during the Lifestream sequence. During his flashbacks, Cloud admits that when he was a child, he wanted to become someone else—namely, Sephiroth.

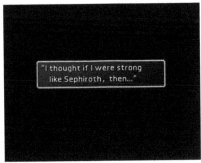

Cloud's psychotic impersonation of Zack makes a little more sense in light of this information. Cloud has always wanted to be like someone else. He chose someone famous for strength, someone the world at large admired. He may not have chosen poorly because that implies a foresight that is impossible; rather, Cloud chose unfortunately.

What if your idol came to your hometown and killed (or nearly killed) everyone you love? The violence of that act alone is enough to cause someone to snap, but Cloud also idolized Sephiroth, adding the feeling of betrayal to an already gruesome murder.

There's a deeply bitter irony in Cloud's connection to Sephiroth which helps to explain the depth of this betrayal, and why Cloud has to defeat Sephiroth in order to truly be himself. As a child and adolescent, Cloud wanted to be like Sephiroth. After Sephiroth nearly kills him, Cloud gets his wish, much more literally than he ever imagined. In the flashback that takes place in the Shinra Mansion basement, we see Cloud emerge from one of the tanks with Zack after being infused with Jenova cells—the same essence that gives Sephiroth his power. Unfortunately, this also gives Sephiroth/Jenova the power to control Cloud at the Temple of the

Ancients and in the Whirlwind Maze. It probably also explains what's happening during the very last battle of the game.

If there is a plot-related explanation for this event, it's probably that Cloud is defeating the Sephiroth inside of him—literally and symbolically. On the literal level, Cloud's body is the last significant source of living Jenova cells anywhere near the Northern Crater, and would thus be Sephiroth's last chance to complete his plan. On the symbolic level, Cloud is exorcising the last remnant of the person he wanted to be—the person who hurt him the most in his life. Cloud's defeat of Sephiroth is still an act of vengeance—there's no way around that fact. It's also more than that; ridding the world of Sephiroth is also the only way that Cloud can be himself, both literally and figuratively. Of course, it also saves the world.

Villains

Villains in *FFVII* embody the survivor's trio as well. The two major villains, Sephiroth and Rufus, are quite different in the way they relate to survivorship. To illustrate what I mean by this, I'll give an example from a minor villain: Dyne. Barret's confrontation with Dyne illustrates the meaning of the survivor's trio succinctly. Dyne survived the same event Barret did, but had the opposite reaction. Whereas Barret is on a mission to save the world (albeit through deeply unethical means), Dyne is on a mission to destroy the world.

Dyne's observation is a keen one. Marlene is a child, and as such, she is naturally resilient and will build an identity around the life she's currently living. Dyne can probably never be connected to her, and he knows it. Lacking a connection, he wants to kill everyone and everything. Barret is willing to kill as well, but the scope of his vengeance is smaller and his ultimate goal is to save the world (rather than destroy it) so that Marlene can grow up and live in it.

Rufus, the game's second-biggest antagonist, is the antithesis of the survivor's trio. Because he's so self-absorbed and arrogant, he actually explains his own nature to the party clearly and immediately upon arriving. Nobody explains Rufus quite like Rufus.

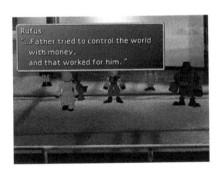 

He's not a survivor in a world that doesn't have a place for him. Rufus is an heir to a world that will do what he wants it to do. It doesn't matter what the current state of the world is; Rufus is going to change it to suit himself. He's never had a near-death event—in fact, no one has ever seen him so much as bleed. He avows no connection to the past (willfully ignoring the means of his inheritance). Indeed, he appears to be on a mission to re-shape everything that came before him into a world he envisions, because he disdains the way things used to be done. In other words, Rufus is the opposite of the protagonists.

Sephiroth, on the other hand, represents an extreme version of survivorship that leads him to evil. He checks off all the boxes in the survivor's trio: he lacks the world that defined him, he has a near-death experience, and he has something that connects him to the past. It's just that each point in the trio is extreme for Sephiroth. Although he has a human body, Sephiroth is much like a resurrected fossil, made from the cells of an organism that has been dead—or at least sealed away—for two thousand years. While some of the protagonists are a few decades removed from the context that defined them, Sephiroth is separated from the world that would have defined him by millennia.

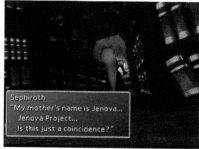

Once Sephiroth believes that he should have belonged to a bygone era, he goes on a murderous rampage. His near-death experience—and his reaction to it—are just as extreme. After first being impaled by Cloud, he's tossed into the very dangerous Lifestream, but he doesn't suffer any ill effects from it at all. Instead, Sephiroth actually gets stronger and even more bloodthirsty. It's not enough to merely kill the residents of Nibelheim. Sephiroth wants to kill everyone other than himself by literally ending the world—a scenario in which he will be the only survivor.

Sephiroth's connection to his past comes through Jenova, his "mother," who finally gets to achieve her goal of consuming the world's biosphere through him. In a certain sense, Jenova is like Rufus; she will remake the world in her own image, although in a much more primal sense of the word. Rufus wants to rule others; Jenova wants to absorb/infect them. (There's no obvious separation between what Jenova wants and what Sephiroth wants.)

Hojo later adds that Jenova's body always recomposes itself over time, reforming and returning to its mission. Jenova is the context that never truly dies, a past that never disappears, a cancer that is always relapsing. That Sephiroth is willing to accept an identity as a part of such a being in order to feel that he is a part of something is very grim (and it taxes belief in retrospect), but it does fit neatly with the theme of the game.

Although I haven't yet attempted it for any other character, I want to make an additional defense of the character of Sephiroth. *Final Fantasy VII's* main villain has long been an important target of its critics. There seems to be a popular memory of Sephiroth as a ghoulish caricature of a super-villain, laughable in hindsight. (Some of this stems from his poor secondary characterization in later media like *Kingdom Hearts* and *Advent Children*.) His megalomania does indeed reach an absurd peak; he wants to kill everyone in the world in order to become a god. It's easy to understand why such a goal can be perceived as melodramatic: it lacks human scale. Kefka, the main villain of *FFVI*, is also an omnicidal maniac, but he doesn't receive as much criticism for it because of his human flaws. Kefka is inconsistent, disorganized, and genuinely vulnerable (although wholly unsympathetic) at several points in the game. Sephiroth, by contrast, seems to be an untouchable opponent whose every plan works out perfectly the first time. When I replay the game, I too find his success to be a little too easy. On the other hand, I wonder if this reaction is a product of our collective prejudices against JRPG villains, rather than being the product of a poor characterization of Sephiroth. Very few JRPG villains are genuinely or consistently intelligent. Other Squaresoft villains have their moments: Exdeath (*FFV*) waits until his opponents are at their weakest to make his move. Kefka has the brutal clarity to know he can get away with genocide as long as Gestahl needs him. Ultmecia (*FFVIII*) is an adept enough student of history to know exactly whom to manipulate to gain political power in a different era. Kuja (*FFIX*) cunningly selects Brahne as the ideal aggressor in a war that benefits himself. The rest of the time, however, these villains succeed based on players and player characters being ignorant of their machinations. How many times in a JRPG does the player's party fight their way through a dungeon only for the antagonists to simply appear, thank them for their labor, and steal the prize? Or how often is there an ancient secret whose nature is quite easily understood when one has all the proper information, but the villain is the only one who has that information? Worst of all, how often does a villain's power or intelligence fluctuate wildly when it's convenient for the plot? The repetition of these tropes has biased us against displays of intelligence from villains generally, and JRPG villains in particular.

Sephiroth is extremely intelligent, and is characterized as such on a very consistent basis. It would almost be absurd of the *FFVII* team to characterize him as anything but intelligent considering the backstory they made for him. He is the superhuman child of two brilliant researchers, and from the very beginning of his introduction to the party, his intelligence and affinity for science are clear.

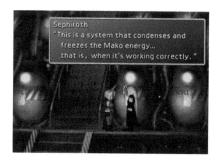 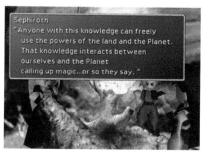

Note that he isn't struggling with any of the technical terms or merely repeating something he read in a manual. Sephiroth gives us his understanding of Shinra science in a casual vernacular. He is even familiar enough with the personnel of the science department to (accurately) judge the relative merits of professor Gast and Hojo. He figures out almost everything that went on in the Shinra Mansion and Nibelheim reactor in a few days. Although his superhuman strength and stamina obviously allow him to do things other humans cannot do, his mind also appears to be capable of great feats as well.

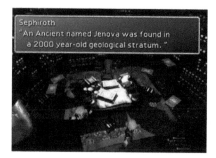 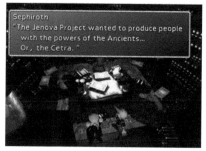

Sephiroth comes to the wrong conclusion at first, but only because he doesn't know what Ilfana eventually told professor Gast. In that sense, he is the very opposite of a typical villain. A typical villain has access to secret knowledge, but often seems inept at actually putting that knowledge to use. Sephiroth has wrong and incomplete knowledge, but he comes very close to the truth because of his excellent comprehension. It's easy to dismiss Sephiroth's rantings as a convenient way to deliver some exposition and move the plot. That misses the ongoing characterization of Sephiroth as dangerously intelligent. In the crater, when Sephiroth realizes that it might not benefit him to fight the whole party and the incoming Shinra forces all at once, he manipulates Cloud and Tifa quite deftly. Although the graphics of *FFVII* were among the best of its time, they weren't perfect. It's easy to miss that during Sephiroth's speech to Cloud and Tifa they are surrounded by the mutilated bodies of the Nibelheim villagers, like the one on the left in the screenshots below.

Making manipulative speeches over the bodies of dead loved ones takes an understanding of human connections and their meaning. This should puncture any image we have of Sephiroth as an inhuman evil. He understands, as well as any *Final Fantasy* villain before or since, human weakness and how to exploit it. He's a terrible person, but his personhood is still a major factor in his characterization through most of the plot.

3

Quantitative Analysis of the Game Script

The form of a narrative always has a significant effect on the way that narrative is told. Whether the narrative in question is an epic poem, a one-act drama, or a videogame, there are practical concerns that will shape the narrative in meaningful ways. This chapter compares the structure of the dialogue in FFVII to the structure of the dialogue in *The Great Gatsby*. Neither *FFVII* nor F. Scott Fitzgerald's novel should be taken as perfectly representative of the forms they employ to tell their stories, but the comparison between them still reveals quite a few meaningful things about the nature of storytelling in general, and dialogue in particular. I chose *The Great Gatsby* as a point of comparison for two primary reasons. First, the two texts are quite close in terms of length. The script of *Final Fantasy VII* and the full text of *The Great Gatsby* both run about 45,000 words. Secondly, the novel deals with very similar themes to those in *FFVII*. Jay Gatsby tries to be someone he's not in order to recreate a past that may not really have happened the way he remembers it. This statement could be said about Cloud almost word for word, but is also fairly applicable to Barret, Yuffie, Vincent, Sephiroth, and several other characters. The way that the dialogue in each breaks down, however, is different, and that's where things get interesting.

37

The most basic structural concerns are important here: the *FFVII* script I counted from included only dialogue, totaling 43,903 words.[34] The version of *The Great Gatsby* that I used (the University of Adelaide's online eBook version) includes dialogue and Nick Carraway's narration. For this analysis, I was only interested in the dialogue from *Gatsby*, which totaled just under 13,000 words.[35] This does make the comparison unequal on a basis of total words, but it doesn't hurt the rate statistics that make up the bulk of this analysis. There are two other basic structural differences that should be noted from the outset. The first is that *Gatsby* has chapter divisions, which were a feature put into the book by Fitzgerald himself. Chapters are, obviously, a common feature of novels, although different authors use them to divide their books differently. Fitzgerald usually begins a new chapter when there is a significant change in time in his narrative. The most common cause for a chapter break is the transition from a night party to the morning or day after. *Final Fantasy VII*, on the other hand, has quests. In many games—even some by Squaresoft—the quests are defined explicitly.

Final Fantasy VII gives no such explicit subdivision, but the general formula for a JRPG quest is now and has historically been that a quest consists of a (1) new town, (2) new dungeon, and (3) boss fight. *Final Fantasy VII* sticks to this formula fairly consistently (Table 3.1).

Table 3.1 Quest Elements in *Final Fantasy VII*

Quest	Town	Dungeon	Boss
First Reactor	Sector Seven Slums	Reactor Interior	Guard Scorpion
Second Reactor	None	Tunnels/Reactor	Air Buster
The Flower Girl	Sector Five Slums	Sector Five/Six Paths	None
Wall Market	Wall Market	None	Aps
The Pillar	None	Sewers, Graveyard	Reno
Shinra Break-in	Wall Market (update)	Shinra Building	Sample HO512
Shinra Break-out	None	Shinra Building	Hundred/Heli Gunner, Motorball
Flashback at Kalm	Kalm/Nibelheim	Mt Nibel (brief)	None
To Junon	Chocobo Ranch	Mithril Mines	Bottomswell
Crossing	Upper Junon	Cargo ship	Jenova BIRTH
To Corel	Costa del Sol	Mt Corel	None
Corel Prison	Gold Saucer	Corel Prison	Dyne
Gongaga	Gongaga	Jungle, Reactor	Reno, Rude
Cosmo Canyon	Cosmo Canyon	Cave of the Gi	Gi Nattak
Nibelheim	Nibelheim	Shinra Mansion, Mt Nibel	Materia Keeper
Rocket Town	Rocket Town	None	Palmer
Wutai	Wutai	Da-Chao Statues	Rapps
Temple of the Ancients	None	Temple of the Ancients	Red Dragon, Demon's Gate
City of the Ancients	Bone Village	Coral Valley (brief)	Schizo, Jenova Death
The Execution	None	Junon Admin Offices	None
Finding Cloud	Mideel	None	None
Materia Train	North Corel	Materia Train	None (Eagle Gun?)
Fort Condor	Fort Condor	None	Cmd Grand Horn
The Launch	Rocket Town	None	Rude
Lifestream	None	None	None
Underwater Reactor	Upper Junon (new)	Underwater Reactor	Carry Armor
Holy	Cosmo Canyon	None	Diamond Weapon
Return to Midgar	None	Tunnels/Sister Ray	Turks, Proud Clod, Hojo
Northern Crater	None	Northern Crater	Jenova Synthesis, Sephiroth

There are a few places where the *Final Fantasy* designers play with the traditional JRPG formula. There's no boss fight in the escape from Junon after the Weapon attack. Instead, Scarlett and Tifa have a slap fight on the end of a cannon at the exact moment where one might expect a boss fight. The quest to find Cloud (immediately after escaping Junon) doesn't have a boss fight, nor does it have a dungeon, although it could easily be combined with the train headed toward North Corel and its several boss-like fights to represent one whole quest. I don't make that combination because the objectives are so different, but the gameplay elements line up perfectly. The quest to go with Bugenhagen to find out what happened with Aeris and Holy doesn't have a town or dungeon, but it does have a kind of scavenger hunt to find the ancient key device, and it does have a boss. This is short, but it still provides a bit of the exploration a dungeon would have provided. All of these exceptions are not omissions, but rather are examples of the designers deliberately playing with the formula to keep the game from becoming repetitive. This is like the technique of deliberately deviating from a rhyme scheme or metrical foot in a poem in order to convey extra meaning or alter the mood. The tension between form and freedom is what makes the poem or JRPG interesting.

With the larger structural differences now set aside, I want to look at how the dialogue is meted out across both narratives to see what smaller structural differences emerge. On a simple words-per-chapter/quest basis, there are some pretty clear differences.[36,37]

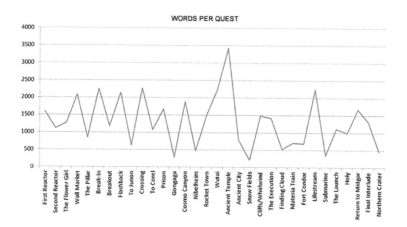

3. Quantitative Analysis of the Game Script

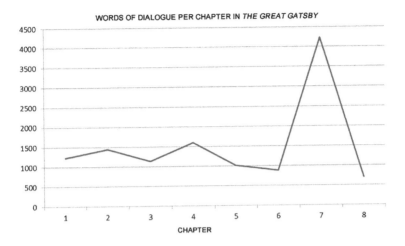
WORDS OF DIALOGUE PER CHAPTER IN *THE GREAT GATSBY*

What they have in common is a clear peak. The emotional climax of *The Great Gatsby* is where one would expect it—towards the end in Chapter 7—and the largest amount of dialogue occurs right along with it. The emotional climax of *FFVII* is definitely not at the Temple of the Ancients, however, so the abundance of dialogue there is something of a puzzle. There are two factors that probably cause the dialogue to peak there. The Temple of the Ancients fits well into a trope known as the "Disc One Final Dungeon," or, as I prefer to call it, the first climax of the game. (This type of dungeon doesn't always appear on disc one of a multi-disc game. In fact, the widespread use of multiple discs was a fairly short-lived phenomenon.) Squaresoft RPGs featured this trope quite often: the Floating Continent, Exdeath's Castle, Magus's Castle, etc. In many cases, the enemies in such a dungeon are suddenly more powerful, and dispense more EXP, ability points, money, and items. The bosses in these dungeons tend to have much more HP (although they're not necessarily much harder) and their own unique battle music, making for longer and more memorable fights. Accordingly, it makes sense that along with the first climax of all the statistical design elements, the dialogue might increase in quantity as well. Why doesn't the peak in quantity come at the emotional peak of the game? This probably has to do with the structure of a videogame story. In the Temple of the Ancients, the writers reveal the long-term backstory of the game—Sephiroth's plan, Aeris's lineage, the planet's history, and so on. Fitzgerald might be telling a complex story in *Gatsby*—full of artistic nuance and complex psychology—but it's nevertheless a very simple plot about an affair between a bootlegger and his married ex-girlfriend. Nobody in *Gatsby* ever has to stop and explain a bunch of invented metaphysical concepts. That, and much of the backstory in *Gatsby* (which is actually considerable) is explained in narration, not dialogue. Different story structures naturally lead to different statistical distributions in dialogue.

Knowing how many words there are in a chapter or quest does not give us a total understanding of how *FFVII* and *The Great Gatsby* differ in narrative structure. We have to delve into finer statistical points to figure that out. One thing I examined was the number of words per line in each text, and I found that those numbers revealed some meaningful trends.[38,39]

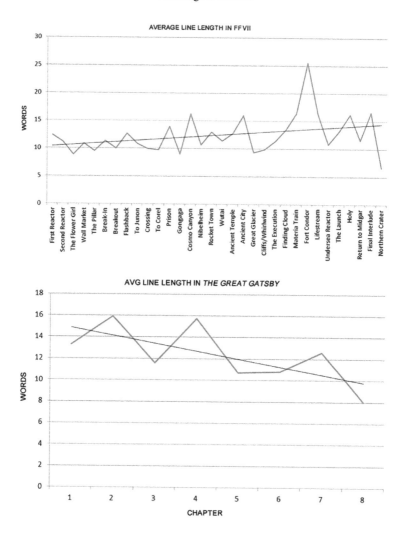

Note that I use a special definition of the word line. A "line" of dialogue has a specific historical meaning (coming from verse dramas) and a current technical meaning (for union pay-scales), but for my purposes, I define a line as being the amount of words said before something or someone interrupts the speaker.

For *Gatsby*, I did not count narrations like "he said" as interruptions, nor did I count adjectival descriptions of the speech. Only a narrated action—or an interruption by another speaking character—counted as an interruption. For *FFVII*, the criteria are dependent on the visual and interactive interruptions, like battles, cinema scenes, or movement controlled by the character. In any case, the stats show opposite trends in the length of lines in the two texts. Although the overall amount of dialogue goes down across the course of *FFVII*, the lines tend to get a little bit longer. (The absurd peak in Fort Condor comes from the unnamed NPC explaining the minigame's rules, assuming the player has never been there before.) There is a lot of variation in line length between quests, although there's an overall trend of longer lines as the game goes on. It's not a terribly strong trend as the trendline shows, but it's there. *Gatsby* is quite different; the lines go down in length clearly, and you can see on the trendline how pronounced a trend it really is.

What should we make of the change in line lengths? Why do the speakers in *FFVII* become slightly more loquacious over the course of the game while those in *The Great Gatsby* become clearly terser toward the end of the book? I think that the answers for each have reasons that relate directly to the form of the narrative. Long speeches or story segments can alienate a certain part of the gaming audience, as we have seen time and time again. *Final Fantasy VII* is able to support longer speeches at the end of the game because players who have reached that point are invested in the characters, in beating the game, or both. Meanwhile, the marked drop in line length in *Gatsby* comes from a structural facet of the novel. Although there are three acts of violence in the novel, two of which are described directly by the narrator (and happen to the same unfortunate person), the book does not spend many words on them. When Tom breaks Myrtle's nose, for instance, the entire act is related to us in 14 words, whereas a sentence describing a dog watching a party in the paragraph before this event is described in 22 words. Most of the "action" of Fitzgerald's novel isn't narrated violence, but rather exists in the interpersonal conflict, specifically in the dialogue. It makes a lot of sense that the dialogue would become shorter and more quippish when two people are facing off against one another verbally, which is exactly what happens in the climactic chapters. This short, combative dialogue does for *Gatsby* what the actual battles do for *FFVII*. Thus, it explains the drop in line length towards the end of *Gatsby* and the smaller overall amount of text in the last quests of *FFVII*.

Another way to look at the structure of the dialogue in *FFVII* and *The Great Gatsby* is to look at who does the most speaking, and how those characters speak. The top five speakers in both narratives do a lot of the speaking, as we might expect.[40,41]

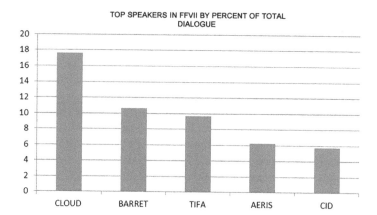

TOP SPEAKERS IN FFVII BY PERCENT OF TOTAL DIALOGUE

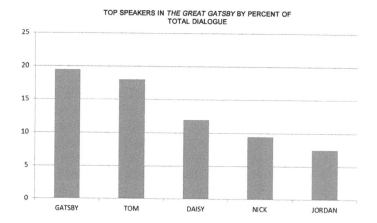

TOP SPEAKERS IN *THE GREAT GATSBY* BY PERCENT OF TOTAL DIALOGUE

The top five speakers in *Gatsby* speak 66% of the words, while those in *Final Fantasy VII* speak 49% of the words. *Gatsby* has an obvious advantage in that those five characters are the main characters of a story with a relatively small cast. There are many ancillary characters at Gatsby's parties, but few of them are ever developed in any meaningful way. The top five speakers in *Final Fantasy VII* speak about half the dialogue in the game, but their contribution is somewhat diluted by the large roster of named NPCs who speak about 29% of the total dialogue. If we count the dialogue of every party member in *FFVII* and not just the top five speakers, we get a figure of 59% of the total dialogue, which is closer to the amount of dialogue spoken by the main characters of *Gatsby*, although still seven percentage points away.

There are plenty of smaller differences between the two narratives in the top speakers' data. Cloud and Gatsby, the protagonists of either tale, speak a comparable amount of the dialogue—17% and 19%, respectively. After that,

3. Quantitative Analysis of the Game Script

the comparison reveals something interesting: Tom Buchanan speaks almost as much as Gatsby, and far more than any *FFVII* antagonist does. Without looking at the cold, hard numbers, I never would have realized just how much time Fitzgerald spends on comparing the self-made Gatsby with his old-money antithesis. Between them, they speak almost a third of the novel's dialogue. Sephiroth, by contrast, speaks a little more than 4% of the dialogue of *FFVII* (making him the sixth top speaker in the game). This, too, is somewhat structural; Sephiroth is present in a very small number of scenes. Much like Kefka in *FFVI*, he is immured in his final dungeon for the latter portions of the game. He also never speaks another word after manipulating Cloud into delivering the Black Materia. I think this presentation of the antagonist is judicious, however. Sephiroth is a supervillain and would become less menacing (and more cartoonish) if he appeared too often and spoke too much. Tom Buchanan is despicable, but he's just a man, and his humanness permits him more time in the spotlight than Sephiroth can afford.

Finally, I think it is useful to examine how long each main character's lines are in both *FFVII* and *Gatsby*. This is less an exercise in structure than in style. If we were to look at the line lengths in Hemingway or Austen novels, we might see that the characters in those books offer a tremendous contrast with what we see from the characters in *Gatsby*. That said, the comparison still tells us something about the difference between RPG characters and novel characters.[42,43]

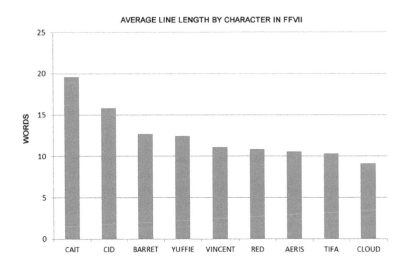

AVERAGE LINE LENGTH BY CHARACTER IN FFVII

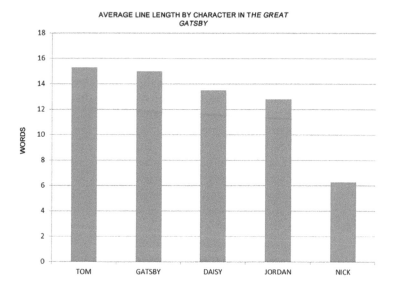

AVERAGE LINE LENGTH BY CHARACTER IN *THE GREAT GATSBY*

Tom and Gatsby are fairly comparable in terms of length. Daisy and Jordan are reasonably close to each other, too, although they are significantly less verbose than their male counterparts. Nick is quite laconic, although that's an important part of his personality that he himself remarks upon more than once. The characters in *FFVII* don't really have as much parity, even if divided into groups. Like Nick in *Gatsby*, Cloud speaks the shortest average lines of the main characters. In this case, it's probably not a function of his characterization as much as it is a function of the many times where he has obligatory, short lines like "Huh?" or "Yeah," or "Sephiroth!?" Those lines have an important function of standing in for the player's decisions or setting the mood of a scene when the graphics might not be fully up to the task. If we look at the other characters in FFVII, some of it doesn't seem to make sense. Is Cait Sith really that verbose? Well, yes he is, but he also only speaks a little over 2% of the game's lines, so his few long-ish speeches will skew the average. Cid speaks about twice as many lines as Cait Sith, and his totals are much closer to the rest of the party. He only has two "speeches" as such, but he also doesn't have many short quips. Cid only speaks ten one-word lines (Cloud speaks more than 80, Barret more than 20), and only seven two-word lines. Thus, his two longer speeches in the rocket and later in the airship can bloat his average pretty significantly. For the most part, everyone from Barret through Cloud is pretty close together in terms of how long their average lines are.

For amateur JRPG designers, who seem to be more and more numerous these days, I want to put in a little bit about how characterization affects dialogue statistics. Although I do not hope to persuade anyone about the artistic effectiveness of this tactic, I find that many of the characterizing moments in *FFVII* are quite subtle. For instance, when Tifa meets Rufus for the first time, she remarks that he "likes to make speeches, just like his father." Tifa's quick derision gives us an alternative to Barret's loud-mouthed hatred of Shinra. Tifa's observation is an interesting one, however, because the data tell a different story. President Shinra is verbose; his average line length is just a little above seventeen words—more words than any main character speaks per line (and that's with Barret constantly interrupting him every time he tries to talk). Rufus begins with a speech, but that speech is essentially about his Machiavellian plan for his inherited empire. Rufus actually speaks about 13 words per line, which is much closer to the average of 12 words spoken by main characters than it is to his father's longer average length. The real speech-making villain is, naturally, Sephiroth, who clocks in at about 20 words per line. Interestingly, before his villainous transformation in Nibelheim, Sephiroth only speaks about 16 words per line. After his breakdown, his lines get a lot longer, so there's a correlation between omnicidal mania and line length for him.

Correlations, as statisticians tell us, do not necessarily imply causation; there is another possible explanation for the lengthier speeches of President Shinra and Sephiroth. The need for exposition drives longer speeches, if Bugenhagen is any example. Aeris is a living embodiment of history, but because she is mostly unaware of that history, Bugenhagen has to give the party most of the background information about the Cetra and the Lifestream. His dialogue (monologues, really) reflect this; Bugenhagen speaks an average of 23 words at a time, higher than any other named character. It shouldn't be surprising, then, to find that after Bugenhagen and Sephiroth, Hojo is number three on the list of longest average lines.

Spirit energy is the source of life for trees, birds, and humans.

"I offered the woman with my child to Professor Gast's Jenova Project."

Bugenhagen explains the way the planet works, and Hojo explains the way that Jenova works. Sephiroth, meanwhile, is completely hung up on himself and his own plan, but then he would be, wouldn't he?

Overall, what we see is that the distribution of dialogue tends to follow the structural concerns of the narrative. I should say that the preceding statement is one that really ought to be backed up by statistical research on a much larger number of videogames and novels, but such a task is outside the scope of this project. For the two narratives in question, it does seem that argument is the medium of conflict in *The Great Gatsby*, and so the dialogue grows shorter as the conflict grows more intense. *Final Fantasy VII* shows no especially strong trend, with only a slight uptick in the length of lines as the game goes on. The discrepancy in speakers—the main characters of *Gatsby* speak a larger proportion of the lines than their videogame counterparts—is certainly a product of *FFVII* having so many more named (and important) characters, as JRPGs often do. Certainly, an author or game designer could choose to produce an avant-garde narrative that defies structural conventions, but I suspect that this is not terribly common.

NPC Dialogue

Like every *FF* title before it, *FFVII* features a script that is longer than that of the previous game in the series. The growth of the length of scripts in the *FF* series is a gradual one; each script is a few thousand words larger than the previous one. The growth in NPC dialogue between *FFVI* and *FFVII*, on the other hand, is explosive. There are around 280 unique NPC interactions in *FFVI*. There are more than 1,050 such interactions in *FFVII*. (In both cases, it depends on what you count as NPC dialogue, although I'll go over my methodology below.) Not only are there more reactions to be found in *FFVII*, but the raw amount of words spoken by NPCs is also quite high. The script of *FFVII* runs just over 43,900 words, while there are more than 26,000 words of NPC dialogue in the game—more than half the length of the game script. Although it's easy for hasty players to miss a lot of this dialogue, the team that created *FFVII* put a lot of energy into making NPCs a meaningful part of their fictional world.

The presence of all those speaking NPCs begs the question: what are they there to do? In a traditional open-world RPG, NPCs are an important source of quests, or at least information about where to find quests. This is largely what NPCs in *FFVI* did, too, because that game had an open second half, and NPCs acted as signposts to the various dungeons that appeared in the World of Ruin. In *FFVII*, however, this role is diminished because the non-linear parts of the game are few in number and are almost all at the end. This doesn't mean that NPCs have nothing important to do; that's exactly the kind of misunderstanding that people have held about the design of *FFVII* for nearly two decades now. The NPCs of *FFVII* are a reflection of the designers' focus on plot, character development, and world building more than anything else. The statistical analysis that follows shows exactly how this emphasis plays out in measurable terms.

NPC Irony and NPC Sociology

It's not enough to know that the most common activity for *FFVII*'s NPCs is to serve in embellishing the fiction of their world. It's also important to understand how they do this, and what else they do when they're not doing their most common activity. To study NPCs, I use a framework of two ideas: NPC irony and NPC sociology. (If you've read *Reverse Design: Final Fantasy VI*, you're already familiar with this framework, although there are a few new nuances that have developed over time.) NPC irony is a way of explaining how the designers of the game communicate necessary information to their players without breaking the narrative spell of the game. Irony means that a speaker's meaning is something other than the literal interpretation of what he or she is saying. NPC irony is the designer's way of giving the player instructions through an NPC without literally having to give them instructions. A good example of this occurs during the party's break-in at Shinra HQ. The party is locked out of the conference room where Shinra executives are having an important meeting. The other NPCs on the floor give them clues as to how they can listen to it.

Everything these NPCs say is written in an in-universe style. These are plausible comments for office workers to be making, but they also tell the player what to do. The elegance of NPC irony comes from the designer's ability to tell the player what to do without having to break the fiction of the game. Players can stay immersed in the world and still learn everything about the game that they need to know. There are hundreds of examples of NPC irony in *FFVII*, and several different subtypes of ironic communication that serve different purposes.

NPC sociology is simply the process of counting up and explaining with statistics the various types of interactions the player has with NPCs. Along with ironic communications from the designer, there are also unironic NPC interactions that serve to develop the world, plot and characters. Below is a list of the types of NPC communications common to the *Final Fantasy* series, with explanations and examples of their usage.

Ironic Communication

Direction: This type of communication consists of more-or-less blatant instructions from the designer to the player. The hallmark of NPC direction is that it tells players everything they need to know to make their next move. This type of communication comes in varying strengths of irony; some instances of it are explicit to the point of being a manual, while others are written in a much more in-universe manner.

In the example here, the NPC makes it very clear that he saw Sephiroth head off toward the grasslands area, which is the next stop on the main quest. It's obvious what the player needs to do. In every case, the required action is clear, and the player has all the necessary information to pursue it.

Allusion: Allusion is like direction in that it presents the player with some direct instructions to do something. The key difference for an allusion is that it deliberately leaves out some important information. In this sense, it's like a puzzle version of a direction.

These NPCs give the player information about people, places, and things, but the player has to interpret the clues and use their own background knowledge and puzzle-solving skills to complete the described task. The Chocobo Sage wavers between this and direction. Although his clues get more specific as he remembers them, he always leaves out exact locations so that the player has to search around. The Kalm Traveler is also deliberately vague. The Guidebook is located in the underwater reactor sea tunnel, morphed from a monster that looks like a ghost ship. This is a really tough allusion because "going down with the ship" sounds a lot like the Gelnika. In the age of Google, it's hard to imagine how much satisfaction a player could have gotten by figuring that out themselves.

Condition: Sometimes a designer needs to tell a player not to pursue something, and in that case, they generally have an NPC communicate a condition. I use the term condition in the sense of "the condition of an object" and not the sense of "I agree under certain conditions." Essentially, NPCs will tell you that the condition of an object, area, or person is "off limits." The player cannot access the thing, and there is nothing he or she can do to access it except to come back later. The big difference between conditions and directions/allusions is that the player doesn't receive any instruction except for "not right now." If the NPC in question can be circumvented by some action, then his communication is a direction or allusion instead.

3. Quantitative Analysis of the Game Script

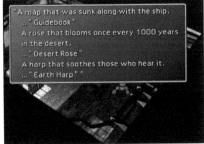

Conditions in *Final Fantasy*, and in most games, are almost always negative or non-use conditions. That is, they tell the player that some object, location, or person will become available later, but isn't available now. That's necessary, and I'm glad those communications exist in games, but it's strange to me that there are so few examples of the reverse. There are plenty of instances in a game where a person, place, or thing in a game is only accessible for a limited amount of time before it disappears forever, but the player is rarely informed of this. A warning that, "Hey, I'm only selling my goods until the festival begins," would technically be a condition. It tells the player that the merchant is available but will become unavailable later. Naturally, the designers don't want to spoil the plot by telling the player that a city is going to be destroyed or something like that, but it's possible to avoid this and still give conditions in reverse order. *Final Fantasy VII* avoids the problem by having very few instances of things that are lost forever. (In *FFVI*, numerous items are lost forever if the player doesn't get them the first time through a dungeon.) That doesn't allow players to make a decision about whether or not they want to pursue the object in question and taking decisions away from players in RPGs is always a risky business.

Non-Ironic Communication

Not all communication through NPCs is ironic. Much of the time, NPCs mean exactly what they say. Instances of non-ironic communication in *FFVII* break down into two categories: elaboration and reaction. Elaborations serve to expand the fictional world of the game by adding details about the people, places, and events that define it. NPCs comment on the nature of characters, provide background details about events in the fictional history of the world, and reflect on the places they inhabit. Reactions, on the other hand, are a class of interaction that depend upon the events of the game. NPCs react to things that happen during the player's quest, reinforcing the importance of those events and the mutability of the game world. After all, the player's agency in that world is one of the things that make videogames different from other media. NPC reactions help to reinforce the player's sense of that agency in an idiosyncratic way.

Elaborations

Person: These NPC interactions give the player extra background information about the major characters of the game. In *FFVII*, most of the examples of this kind of interaction happen in a given character's hometown, such as in the flashback to Nibelheim, the ruins of Corel, or Cosmo Canyon.

One of the artful things about these interactions is that they give the player another view of every character. Most of the characters in *FFVII* have either constructed or attempted to construct new identities to compensate for what they've lost. The NPCS in their various hometowns reveal a more vulnerable and real side of these characters. Cloud's flashback to pre-disaster Nibelheim is a particularly rich source of info on him and Tifa. It also helps to make the villagers feel more persuasive as people, so that their deaths mean something.

Event: This category of interaction expands on events that happened in the universe of the game. Generally, this category applies to events that happened in the fictional past, such as ancient wars or inciting incidents that happened off-screen. The purpose of this interaction is to tell the player something they don't already know rather than simply to provide color commentary on things that the player watched happen.

 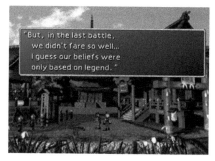

In each case, the player couldn't have seen what the NPCs are talking about, so the player is getting factual information rather than emotional reactions to the event in question. Emotional NPC reactions go into the reaction categories.

Place: This is the most common type of elaboration in *FFVII*, and probably the trickiest to explain fully. A literal example of a reaction in this category involves an NPC describing a place. There are subtler variations as well, however.

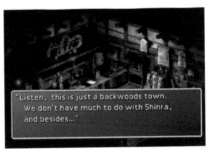

All of the examples are telling the player something about a place, but they don't necessarily have to come out and talk directly about that place. There are many examples of indirect elaborations of place in the game, and some of them can be tricky.

These two NPCs in Wall Market have two fairly long conversations about sifting through garbage from the upper plate. The goal of this conversation is to develop Midgar as the kind of place where someone living in the slums can make a significant living off the refuse that is thrown down from the upper city. They talk a lot about the owner of the weapons shop, but he is not the real subject of their conversation—Midgar is. If the dialogue were truly in the elaboration - person category, it would be about a significant named character, and it would tell us something about that person that the script does not cover. Most of the chatter between NPCs which is neither ironic nor obviously about a named character is in the elaboration - place category. This chatter can sometimes appear purposeless and trivial.

Even triviality—one might say especially triviality—is necessary to make a world feel real. A world that consists only of essential details can feel too robotically ludic and not particularly persuasive. The feeling of actually being in a living, breathing world is the RPG's greatest and most idiosyncratic strength. That is why the balance of ironic to non-ironic chatter favors the latter by a considerable margin, and why elaboration - place is the largest category of all.

Reactions

Situational: Situational reactions are NPC dialogues that refer to an event that transpired during the normal course of the plot, but that do not impart extra plot information about them, and do not blame or credit the player characters for the event. All interactions of the reaction type are emotional and subjective rather than informational. This type of interaction becomes much more prevalent after Sephiroth summons Meteor, but there are lots of reactions to other events as well.

In every case, the NPCs are mulling over the state of the world since an event happened. They don't blame the party for anything (in this category), but they're subject to the same events that the player has seen transpire in the plot. Because the player-characters tend to be the cause of (or at least close to the cause of) these events, this category still reinforces player agency, even if the NPC in question doesn't know the player-character's role.

Attributive: An attributive reaction is any reaction that credits or blames the player for something that happens during the scripted plot of the game.

These are relatively few in *FFVII*, and although I have no performed a large enough survey to claim this for certain, I feel that there are relatively few in JRPGs as a subgenre. After spending 15 hours in *Oblivion* or *Skyrim*, one cannot walk into a town without its residents exclaiming all of the player-character's noteworthy deeds. In JRPGs, this is less common. Several NPCs remark how they think AVALANCHE is the cause of all the world's problems, but that is a result of their own incomplete information and Shinra propaganda as much as any real cause for anger. Moreover, although the player's party includes all of the AVALANCHE leadership, none of the NPCs they encounter recognize them. Instead of reacting to events with a global scope, most of the NPCS who exhibit attributive reactions instead react to some relatively small event that happened immediately in front of them.

Trends in NPC Dialogue

Before diving into the trends of NPC dialogue across the course of the game, I want to address my methodology for counting it. Technically, any character not in the party is an NPC, but I do not count every line of dialogue from a non-party source. Instead, I only count dialogue that is not mandatory for plot progression because the mandatory segments are already counted in the script analysis. For example, Cloud must ascend to the top of Cosmo Canyon and talk to Bugenhagen in order to access the Cave of the Gi, so that is counted as part of the script. If the player returns to Cosmo Canyon after the quest and speaks to Bugenhagen, that's an NPC interaction, and it is counted. The point is not to arbitrarily divide one type of text from another, but rather to avoid counting the same things twice. Another counting method I employed was to count all possible responses an NPC can give when the player has multiple dialogue choices. These choices are almost all on the first disc, and no choice has a serious impact on the game, but they are present, and so I counted them all. Finally, the quest in Wutai is not technically mandatory, but I treated it as though it is, and as such, I did not count the scripted sections that take place there.

Charting Exploration through NPC Dialogue

The raw amount of NPC dialogue per quest provides a good framework for looking at the non-combat aspects of *FFVII*. Chapter 4 of this book details the meticulous pacing of various combat-oriented elements in the game. Generally, the difficulty of dungeons and bosses in *FFVII* moves up and down according to the fundamental principle of videogame design, but we'll cover that in Chapter 4. The amount of available NPC dialogue follows a similar pattern, although for different reasons and not as meticulously. Below is a graph of the amount of NPC dialogue per quest in *FFVII*.

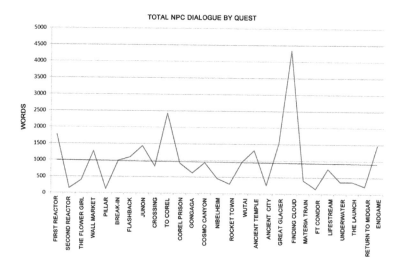

The up-and-down motion of NPC chatter isn't quite as regular as it will be on the more combat-oriented graphs, but it does still follow the pattern. The two peaks in the graph exist for totally different reasons. The first peak occurs in the quest that takes the player from Costa del Sol to North Corel. This quest has a second town in place of a boss fight, and simply has more NPCs as a result. The huge peak (more than 4,000 words) in the "Finding Cloud" quest that takes the party to Mideel is a result of the player's access to the Highwind. The player can go to any town except Midgar, and all of the NPC dialogues have changed now that Meteor has been summoned. It's easy to pass over what a huge effort that is; 4,000 words is a lot to write, but what's really impressive is that there are no repeats at all. All of those new reactions are unique—there are no NPCs who generically remark "I saw a mudcrab the other day." All of these reactions are appropriate for their location and speaker.

What's more, the new NPC chatter isn't just ornamental either (not that it would be a problem, necessarily). Earlier, I praised *FFVII* for its total avoidance of collection quests and other tasks completely unrelated to the plot. One of the ways that the designers can make something like that possible is by using the NPCs to keep the player on track.

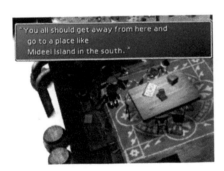
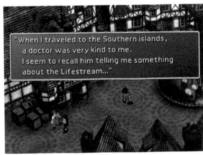

One of the strangely intuitive things about NPC dialogue is that the more NPCs talk about a given topic, the more important that topic will appear to the player. Because NPCs all over the world talk about Mideel, the player should get the hint pretty quickly: fly south. This is a great example of ironic communication, and how NPCs can save the player from having to use a walkthrough.

As was the case with the length of speeches in the script, the length of NPC interactions can tell us a lot about how the *FFVII* dev team used NPCs in their game. There are a few different ways to slice this data, each of which reveals something different. The graph below shows the average length of NPC dialogues per quest.

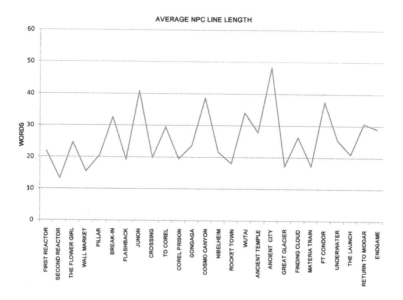

AVERAGE NPC LINE LENGTH

WORDS

Again, we see the up-and-down motion that is completely normal for a videogame. The floor for average NPC interaction stays fairly stable around 18 or 19 words. The peaks, meanwhile, are all over the place, but mostly have mundane explanations. The highest peak (in the quest to get to Junon) is a result of two NPCs: Choco Billy and the headman of Fort Condor.

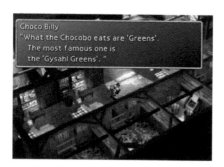

Both of these NPCs give the player long explanations of how to start their respective side quests. That, combined with the fact that there aren't very many NPCs between Kalm and Junon, results in a much higher average words-per-interaction score. The other two peaks are pretty similar, with the return to Fort Condor explaining one, and the explanation of how to detect treasure in Bone Village the other. What's the lesson here? Keep it short. Even long explanations like those don't raise the overall average length for an NPC interaction to more than 24 words (the median length is 17 words). Long explanations of game mechanics are necessary sometimes, and that's okay because it's better to explain too much than too little. Otherwise, if *FFVII* serves as the model for your game, keep NPC speech succinct. If NPCs are going to distribute dozens of small quests, they may have to speak more. If the goal is just to make the game world feel persuasive, NPCs don't need to have a dozen dialogue tree options to accomplish that.

Trends in NPC Irony

Another way to look at NPC dialogue is to sort it out by ironic and non-ironic categories and see how much of each there is, and how many words of each type there are. The former task is fairly easy and gives us perhaps the most single revealing visualization of data about NPCs.

TYPES OF NPC DIALOGUE BY RELATIVE AMOUNT

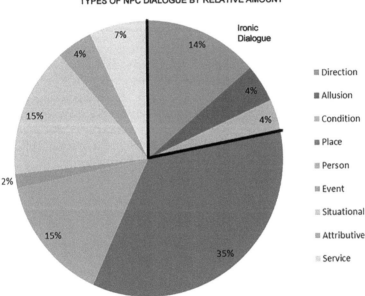

The single largest category is elaboration - place, which makes sense since that category has the broadest scope. It also makes sense that in a game that depends on world-building as much as *FFVII* does, the category that directly serves that world-building would have the most chatter in it. The largest ironic category by far is direction. The amount of direction chatter is much higher in *FFVII* than it was in *FFVI* (although fairly comparable to *Chrono Trigger*). The probable cause of this is the many minigames and extra mechanics that have to be explained. Most RPGs tell the player how to play the basic game through NPCs, but *FFVII* also has to teach the player how to ride and breed chocobos, fight in the battle arena, and play all those neat games in the Gold Saucer. Accordingly, the direction category is large. This could have been done by an omniscient tutorial, but the *FFVII* team decided to speak through fictional people so as to handle the player's sense of disbelief a little more gently. Considering the game's emphasis on storytelling, this is a sensible artistic decision.

There's a tie for the second largest category, although both of them are of the non-ironic kind. Fifteen percent of the NPC chatter in *FFVII* is elaboration—person, and 15% is reaction—situational. The former category is bog-standard; NPCs in a character's hometown tend to reveal things about their character and past that the player might not otherwise know. For all its radical practices, *FFVII* doesn't do anything that extraordinary with this category. The reaction—situational chatter is more meaningful. Overall, situational reactions make up 15% of NPC chatter, but after Meteor is summoned, they make up 41% of the NPC chatter. Indeed, fully three-quarters of the reaction—situational dialogue that NPCs speak happens after Meteor appears in their sky. The *FFVII* team spent a lot of time and energy showing how the summoning of Meteor affected the residents of the fictional world.

Although I am always hesitant to praise the *FFVII* script for its prosody, it is nevertheless my opinion that the post-Meteor NPC chatter shows a lot of imagination and idiosyncratic artistry that are easy to miss if the player doesn't talk to the NPCs. Whether one likes the plot of *FFVII* is a matter of taste, and in any case, the plot of the game is its least ludic element. Its use of NPCs to embellish the world and plot is, however, a move rooted in the game-design tradition of the great RPGs. The two categories that accomplish this embellishment the best in *FFVII* are the elaboration—place and reaction—situational. The former category does most of its best work early in the game, mostly in Midgar.

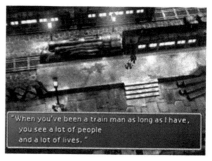

This one NPC does a surprisingly thorough job of talking about the people of Midgar and the city's history. He does it with a lot of emotion, no less, and all in less than 120 words. Quite a few of Sector Seven's inhabitants are similarly effusive.

3. Quantitative Analysis of the Game Script

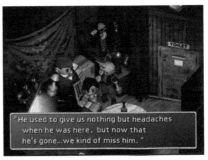

"Ha! Ha!......
I wonder if my son's already left?"

"He used to give us nothing but headaches
when he was here, but now that
he's gone...we kind of miss him."

I think the ostensible goal of dialogues like these is to embellish the realness of Sector Seven, so that when Shinra drops the plate on top of it, the player's sense of loss and outrage will be more acute. The overall amount of NPC speech per quest backs this up; the first quest has the third-most dialogue of any quest. The only two quests with more NPC dialogue are the Corel quest, and the quest to find Cloud—both of which have more than one town to search through, effectively multiplying the amount of NPC dialogue possible. Outside Midgar, there are still quite a few NPCs that expand the player's knowledge of the setting, too.

"No matter how much I pray,
it won't bring our grandson back..."

"Now, it's nothing but a miserable pit!
Me, my bulldozer...everyone's out of work."

Each of these interactions is a particularly good example of the NPC writers reinforcing the main theme of people outliving the death of something that gave them their identity. Communicating a theme through a variety of NPCs is not necessarily a huge accomplishment; the fact that the *FFVII* team is able to do so while maintaining the plausibility of those NPCs is a bit more artful. One of the reasons why it's so easy to miss the thematic content in NPCs is that each of these interactions is perfectly appropriate for the location in which it appears. At first glance, these NPCs appear to be saying standard NPC fare; it is only in seeing the common thread that connects them that the subtleness of the designers' technique becomes clear.

After the summoning of meteor, the type of NPC chatter that the designers use to communicate their theme changes, but the overall effect does not. Just above, I noted that most of the NPC chatter which falls into the reaction category takes place after Meteor has been summoned. That content largely displaces the elaboration content which previously employed most of the game's NPCs. In the definitions section, I explained that the character of reaction content is a little bit different; NPCs use elaboration-category dialogue to make the world feel more real. NPCs use reaction-category dialogue to make the player's actions feel important. In *FFVII*, there's also another difference: when speaking in reactions, the NPCs are often quite imaginative and lyrical.

The image of Meteor reflected on the waves at night is actually quite haunting, if one takes the time to imagine it. It's really a shame that the art team didn't have time to illustrate what the dialogue describes. The NPC standing on his seaplane might be the most perfect possible distillation of the main theme of the game and is also fairly imaginative. He literally wonders aloud where he will go after the world ends. There are dozens of other examples of NPCs having these robustly-imagined reactions to the appearance of Meteor and/or the death of Shinra, Inc. The total NPC dialogue from this category numbers in the thousands of words, and yet many players never even see them. The reason is probably that there's no practical reason to return to many of the world's towns after Meteor is summoned. Those towns mostly don't have any new items or quests to offer, and so there's no occasion for the player to encounter these NPCs. It's a shame that the designers didn't give the player a reason to revisit everything, but quests are expensive and NPC dialogue (especially without voice acting) is cheap.

Game Difficulty and the Four Phases of *FFVII*

In Chapter 1, on the history of the RPG form and *FFVII*'s place in that history, I talked about how the form of an RPG affects its style and content. The transition from the tabletop space to the digital space necessarily caused the design of RPGs to change. We've already seen how the limitations of the digital space—combined with the astonishing completeness of *D&D*—led to RPGs that focused on one or two aspects of the form. There are other changes that arise from the transition to videogame form, and one of them is the adoption of orthodox videogame difficulty structures. Between 1978 and 1986, there was a tremendous amount of evolution in the design of mainstream videogames. *Final Fantasy I* was released in 1987. It only makes sense that FF titles would be influenced by this evolution.

Two ideas form the foundation of videogame design. The first idea is that videogames should generally become more challenging the longer they are played. The second is that this increase in difficulty is not purely linear, but rather goes up and down.[44] Together, the principles describe the phenomenon I call *Nishikado motion*. Nishikado motion is important to the design of *FFVII*, but I want to pay particular attention to the notion that game difficulty should go up and down. *Final Fantasy VII* alternates easier and harder quests throughout the game, and many statistical measures reveal this pattern. With a few exceptions, the difficulty of *FFVII* dungeons features a reliable pattern of tension and release that can be charted clearly. On the other hand, the way in which the designers create a game-long increase in difficulty is much more complicated. The big problem that the *FFVII* designers face when trying to turn up the difficulty across the course of their game was that many of the traditional RPG mechanisms for increasing difficulty don't fit the voice or structure of their game. Tactical party composition had already disappeared in *FFVI* in favor of a party made up of whomever the player wanted to use for plot-and-character reasons. As we'll see, this doesn't leave the design team without tools. Even without tanks, dedicated healers, and fragile spellcasters, the designers have ways of keeping the game interesting. Debuffs, elemental resistances, specially-structured attacks, and changes in enemy base stats are a few of the traditional ways that the designers were able to modify the difficulty of battles. Novel structures in the design of the level-up system are another way of playing with game difficulty. Overall, the game breaks down into four phases, each of which represents a different approach to making the game challenging.

- The first phase is an introduction during which the player learns the game's basic mechanics and can push through most of the content without much critical thinking or knowledge about the game.
- The second phase adds difficulty by inconveniencing the player in various ways over long periods of time, rather than concentrating danger in any one spot.
- The third phase of the game is almost the opposite of the second phase, in that it's all about player characters and their enemies using high-powered attacks.
- The fourth phase of the game combines aspects of phases two and three, but also uses the level-up system in a novel way to create (and solve) difficulty.

Although the transitions between these phases are so smooth that many players miss them, we'll see how the designers managed to pack quite a bit of nuance into *FFVII's* battles and level-up system.

One thing I want to address before diving into the section-by-section analysis is a prejudice that I have encountered many times when doing research on RPGs and JRPGs in particular. There exists a notion that all of the difficulty in a typical JRPG stems from inflation in the base statistics of enemy combatants. That is, JRPG battles become more difficult because monsters have increasingly large HP pools, and attack, and defense stats. This is not really the case with *FFVII*; the truth of its difficulty is much more complicated. In addition to showing that *FFVII* is not the boring, stat-inflation game that some critics think it is, I also want to address the validity of this prejudice in general. There are games that do consist of a long, uphill battle against progressively higher monster stats. *World of Warcraft (WoW)* is one example of this. Although the endgame (raid) content for *WoW* is actually somewhat nuanced and skill-based, most of the content prior to the endgame is simply a series of dungeons and quests that pit the player character against progressively stronger versions of the same old monsters, over and over again. Considering that this part of the game can take 50–100 hours to climb through (although this climb has gotten easier in more recent versions of the game), it's fair to characterize the levelling phase of *WoW* as being exactly the sort of RPG that critics say requires more grinding than skill. *Skyrim* is another game which suffers from stat inflation as the primary means of challenge. The main difference between the enemies at the beginning of *Skyrim* and the enemies at the end is that the later enemies have more HP and better equipment. I am not the first person to point this out, but I think that critics of *WoW* and *Skyrim* tend to admit that judging those games only in terms of their battle systems is to miss the point. *Skyrim* and *WoW* are about more than just finding the next monster to kill. Indeed, most RPGs are about more than finding the next monster to kill. The exploration, atmosphere, character, and storytelling aspects of RPGs are Dave Arneson's enduring contribution to the genre, and ignoring those things is (in most cases) a needlessly reductive exercise.

I have to admit that when I looked at *FFVII's* statistical measures for the first time, I thought I might encounter the kind of inflation that I discuss above, but it wasn't so. The easiest way to prove or disprove this notion is to look at how many physical attacks it would take to end a battle, as this is the most basic action a player can take. Physical attack damage can vary, so for my measure I used Red XIII's physical attack, as he falls roughly into the middle of the damage spectrum. He also joins the party during quest six (breaking into Shinra HQ), which is the point in the game where the party-size stabilizes at three members for the rest of the game. I measured his attack against every enemy, assuming that his character level is equal to the average enemy level for the quest in consideration (rounded down). For every quest in which there was a new weapon available, I figured that weapon into the calculation.[45–48]

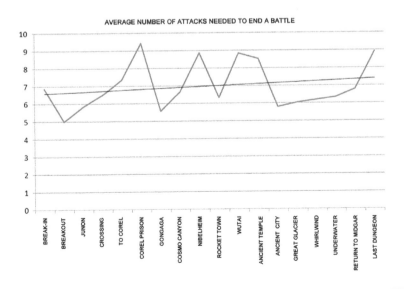

AVERAGE NUMBER OF ATTACKS NEEDED TO END A BATTLE

Over the course of the game, the number of physical attacks required to end a battle does go up slightly. That growth is considerably smaller than I expected, however. Moreover, the way the growth occurs is not in the manner that I expected, either. I did anticipate the possibility of the up-and-down motion of this graph—that some quests would be harder than others based merely on things like HP and defense. The strange thing is that the average number of physical attacks required to end a battle (per quest) never goes much above nine—not for the entire game! I thought that the battles in the hardest quests would require an average of eight attacks, then nine, then 10, then 11, but my hypothesis was wrong. Instead of seeing the hardest quests getting harder (in terms of stats), we see the easiest quests getting harder, while the hardest quests stay the same. The durability of the enemies in the easier quests grows, while the durability of the enemies in the harder quests stays mostly the same (in terms of basic physical attacks).

The fact that the average battle peaks at nine attacks is important, but how I arrived at that average is important as well. The *FFVII* designers appear to have imposed a consistent limit on the average duration of battles (measured in player turns). I don't want to conceal the truth of the data from that graph, however. Each data point represents the average length of a battle per quest. Naturally, there are some battles that are higher than the average, and some battles that are lower. There are some battles whose statistical profile is so extreme that it skews the average of the whole quest. These battles generally fall into two groups: battles with an unusually large number of enemies, and battles with one huge enemy. The former category is about as simple as it sounds in terms of composition. These battles are made up of normal enemies in large quantities, and thus they scale normally in terms of EXP, AP, and everything else. The only really interesting thing about these battles is that they disappear completely just before the Great Glacier quest. By my count, there are 48 random battles (not including chocobo battles) that contain either four or five enemies, but none after the player leaves the Coral Valley. How can we explain this? I think the answer lies in the player's ability to use multi-target attacks. Battles with many normal enemies take a comparable amount of time to finish as battles with one very tough enemy, but only if the player relies entirely on basic physical attacks. The moment a player starts using multi-target abilities, he or she can finish the large-population battles in one or two turns. This isn't true against those beefy enemies, since their HP is concentrated in one spot. As the game goes on, the player's access to powerful multi-target attacks increases markedly, meaning that high-population/low-HP battles would be way too easy for a player who has the Slash-All Materia, or any of the many other skills which can wipe a battlefield clean of weaker foes. The harder enemies prevent the player from abusing multitarget abilities to gain EXP, AP, and gil at a rate that would break the game.

The "beefy enemy" category is a little more interesting from the perspective of individual battle design. The one-tough-enemy setup is typified by the single most durable random encounter in the game: Master Tonberry. The Tonberry appears in many *FF* titles, usually as exactly what he is in *FFVII*—a monster with high HP and some deadly attacks. There's no easy way around the Tonberry; he takes about 35 (average) physical attacks to defeat, and he has no glaring magical weakness to exploit. The Master Tonberry appears as a random encounter in the final dungeon, and so his toughness is completely understandable. There are other enemies like him from many different quests, however. The Blue Dragon of Gaea's Cliffs takes an average of 15 attacks to subdue, while the Dragon of Mt. Nibel requires 13. The X-Cannon from the Return to Midgar requires 18 attacks to defeat, while the King Behemoth in the final quest requires 15. These enemies hand out an average to slightly above-average amount of EXP. The one exception is the Ying & Yang enemy from the Shinra Mansion, which takes a whopping 30 attacks to defeat, but which delivers about 57% less EXP than a typical battle in that zone. The reason is that Ying & Yang are a gimmick battle; one side is nearly immune to physical attacks and the other, magic. This is one of a very small number of gimmick battles in the whole game, but it does skew the data for the Nibelheim/ Mount Nibel area a little bit higher. Thankfully, there are not really any other significant instances of gimmick-based defenses in random encounters, and so the numbers on the physical attacks graph are a fair representation of the game as the player experiences it. (We'll go over this in greater detail in Chapter 6, on enemy archetypes.)

Stat Inflation: Sometimes Meaningful, Sometimes Not

Looking at how many basic attacks go into a battle is the most consistent way to compare enemy durability across quests, as it accounts for level, HP, defense, and even player-character statistics. That said, this method does not account for many of the other stats that enemies (and player characters) have. I expect that the first big question readers have regarding statistical inflation is about the enemy's ability to do damage. Even if the average random encounter lasts no more than nine attacks across the course of the game, what the enemy can do during those turns is pretty important. I want to start out by simply looking at the average stats of enemies on a per-quest basis. Here is a graph of average enemy attack stats, per quest.[49]

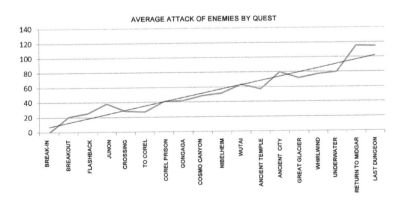

You can see that there's a very strong relationship between quest progression and enemy attack stats. This would seem like a clear indicator of increasing difficulty in the game except that it is mitigated by rising player defenses.[50]

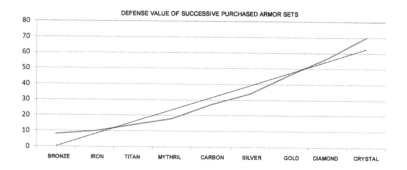

Enemy defenses and player attack power rise similarly, but that data is already baked into the durability graph above, and the relationship is neatly linear. This is a form of stat inflation; it doesn't present the player with much to think about. It does force the player to buy new weapons and armor, and as we'll eventually see, that's meaningful; the acquisition of gil becomes more important during phase four. For most of the game, however, the player simply maintains his or her party's stats in line with the inflation of enemy stats by buying stronger equipment. As far as enemy base damage and armor go, *FFVII* is guilty of boring stat inflation, at least until the final phase when the use of gil becomes a little more interesting. Although physical attacks and defenses inflate somewhat meaninglessly, the same is not true for magic and magic defenses. Enemy magic stats increase in a straightforward, linear fashion.[51]

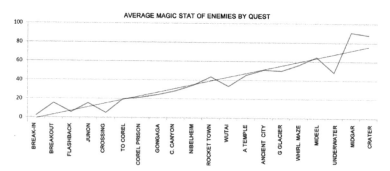

Player magic resistances also rise commensurately, recreating the meaningless inflation of the physical defenses. I have on the graph the physical resistances throughout the game to show how, despite starting lower, the magic resistance on armor catches up to its physical counterpart pretty quickly. What saves the magic/magic defense dynamic from being too boring is that enemy magic defenses are quite a bit different.[52]

Average Magic Defenses of FF7 Enemies per Quest

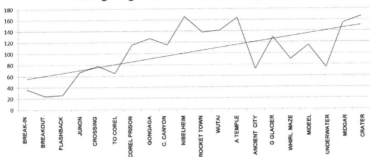

This is the first glimpse we get of the multi-phase structure of the game's difficulty. Indeed, this drop-off in magic defense after the Temple of the Ancients was one of the first indications I had that *FFVII's* difficulty structure could be broken up into distinct phases. That surprising valley in the shape of the magic defense graph is a major part of phase three of the game, which represents a stark and sudden change in the way that battles challenge the player.

Although the mid-game valley in magic defenses is obviously significant, the early zenith of magic defenses is important too. The dialogue analysis shows us a clear "first peak" at the Temple of the Ancients, and the magic defense graph seems to coincide with that. The early peak is typical for a Squaresoft game, and appears in most *FF* titles from the 90s, as well as in *Chrono Trigger*. This peak sits at the end of a long line of quests with high magic defenses, however. Why would earlier enemies be more magic-resistant than later enemies? This question led me to examine the portion of the game which goes from the Shinra Tower until the Temple of the Ancients, and to try to figure out why enemy defense stats would be distributed so counterintuitively. The answer to that question is what revealed the nature of phase two of the game. I'll explain all that in the section on phase two, but the point I want to make here is that most of *FFVII's* statistical dimensions did not show boring, predictable, and linear growth across the course of the game.

Phase One: Introduction

The first phase consists of the first five quests, from the opening bombing mission up through the destruction of the Sector Seven pillar. It is not easy (or helpful) to statistically compare the beginning of *FFVII* to the rest of the game for several reasons. The foremost reason is that the party size is not stable, moving between one and three player-characters across the first five quests. Although party composition is not tactically nuanced in this game overall, the player is frequently forced to carry party members who are under-leveled and underequipped during the first phase. Thus, the difficulty of each battle has to be calibrated to take into account a party of frequently varying size and power. There are many other reasons why this phase can't really be put on the same graphs as other phases. There are relatively few shops during the first phase. The shops that do appear don't offer weapons, armor, or materia as often as they do in later phases. The rate at which the player acquires EXP and AP is different from the rest of the game. In essence, all of the ways in which the player characters would encounter and then master difficulty are different in this phase than they are later on.

Although it's not terribly helpful to compare early statistical trends to the rest of the game in any great detail, the first phase does show the player all of the essential mechanics. Elemental resistances are a good example of this. The player only has basic fire, ice, and lightning spells, but a huge number of enemies are weak against lightning, and so the player has plenty of chances to learn about enemy types and their elemental affinities. Meanwhile, only two enemies in random encounters are immune to a spell the player has. Both of those enemies are located in the Train Graveyard, which is part of the last quest in the phase. The designers are teaching the player through ease and power rather than difficulty and resistance. Similarly, the enemy's use of debuffs is minimal and incomplete. (Debuff is the catch-all term for the family of spells which *Final Fantasy* calls "status effects.") In the first phase of the game, there is only one enemy that can inflict slow, one that can inflict poison and one that can inflict silence. Two enemies can inflict sleep and two can inflict darkness. None of the really dangerous debuffs are present. Moreover, all of these debuff-using enemies are spread out so that no one zone in the first phase is especially rich in debuffs. This is in contrast to the later parts of the game which tend to concentrate debuffs heavily. The designers are introducing game mechanics, but not in a way that is particularly dangerous.

The underlying statistical elements in the beginning section don't compare well with the rest of the game, but there are still some numerical elements that are indicative of the low level of challenge in the beginning of the game. The *FFVII* designers did themselves a huge favor when they constructed the damage formula for enemy combatants. Most of the enemies in the game have an attack that is equal to some multiple of their base attack damage. (I'm going to cover this in much greater detail in phase three, where it's even more relevant.) For example, the formula for the Guard Hound's special attack "Tentacle" is simply base damage*1.5. I call this modifier the component stat, in that it is a kind of contributing statistic that is a component of the ability itself rather than of the character casting it. The component stat is one of the clearest ways in which we can measure increasing difficulty across the course of the game.

In the first phase of the game, most of the component stats for most attacks made by non-boss enemies are below base damage*2. Only two enemies have attacks that equal or exceed that amount. Moreover, there are only two attacks in this phase that can hit multiple targets. Interestingly, the Hell House enemy in Sector Six has the highest damage attack in addition to one of this phase's only multi-target attacks.

 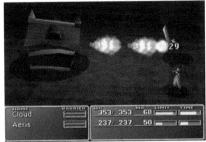

Based on its location in the game, I think that the Hell House's unusual damage output is in place to help Cloud learn his second limit break, but it also serves to teach players that some normal enemies are much more dangerous than others. Most enemies in the first phase aren't like the Hell House. Highly damaging and multi-target attacks will become more prevalent across the course of the game, and players need to know about that. In the first phase, most of the damage dealt by enemies is at or near the levels dictated by enemy base stats. Bosses in the first phase are different from normal enemies, and really, they're also different from bosses throughout the rest of the game. Bosses in *FFVII* tend to have several shared characteristics: large pools of HP and MP, low physical defense, high magic defense, and one or two dangerous attacks that are used infrequently.

Only about a third of bosses in the entire game have an elemental weakness, but all but one of the bosses in the first phase have an elemental weakness. (Of the bosses who do have elemental weaknesses, 60% of them are weak to lightning.) While the high magic defenses of bosses make elemental weaknesses less meaningful, it's still clear that the bosses in phase one are supposed to help teach the player to exploit any advantage. Bosses in phase one also do other unusual things. Many enemies in the game have counterattacks, and sometimes it's not even clear when a counterattack is happening. The Guard Scorpion's counterattack, on the other hand, is actually explained during the battle.

 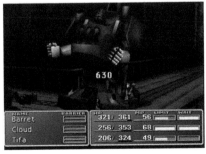

Many enemies and bosses have conditions under which they are more vulnerable, but the Air Buster (the game's second boss) takes six times more damage when it is hit in the back. Many bosses use debuffs that require the player to target the victim with a cleansing ability, but Reno's pyramid technique requires the player to specifically target the debuff itself, which is a great way to force players to think critically about debuffs. Overall, the bosses in the first phase are set up so that the player can see explicit versions of game design ideas that will be subtle in later phases of the game.

Phase Two: Abundant Inconvenience

Phase two of *FFVII* is best characterized by an abundance of small inconveniences for the player characters that don't really present a terrible danger, but that nevertheless make the game feel progressively more challenging. There are three design features that cause these increasing challenges. The first is an abundance of elemental resistances, which peaks surprisingly early in the game. The second is an abundance of low-level debuffs, which peaks around the Temple of the Ancients. The final feature is increases in magic defense, which also peak at the Temple of the Ancients. Although none of these are purely linear (because that would defy the essential voice of videogame design), they do see an overall increase toward a clear climax. In trying to understand the structure of phase two, it's helpful to visualize the enemy's use of debuffs.

Charting the prevalence of debuffs confirms a clear, quantitative "first climax" of which we have already seen evidence of in the textual analysis and magic defense graphs. Below is a graph of debuffs starting from quest six (breaking into Shinra HQ), the point at which party size and party composition stabilize. The graph continues through the final incursion into the Northern Crater.[53,54]

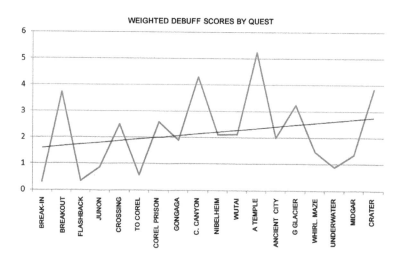

WEIGHTED DEBUFF SCORES BY QUEST

4. Game Difficulty and the Four Phases of *FFVII*

To explain how I came to my conclusions about phases of the game, I want to explain how I represent the data here.

1. The quantity of debuffs is calculated on a per-battle basis, rather than on a per-enemy basis because this is more accurate to the player's experience of the game. Therefore, each data point represents the average number of debuffs that are available to be cast per battle in each of the quests.

2. The graph uses weighted data; some debuffs are worth more than others. Each debuff is weighted based upon the number of turns it costs to remedy. Debuffs like poison, blind, and silence can be removed in one turn by the character who is afflicted by them, and so get a score of one. Debuffs like confuse, paralyze, petrify, and stop consume two turns; the character who is afflicted by the debuff loses a turn while afflicted, and another character spends a turn remedying the debuff. Those debuffs are thusly scored as twos. The only effect scored as a three is instant death because it consumes the turn of the victim, a turn to revive, and a turn to heal the character that was just revived so they don't die again immediately. Many enemy AI scripts are configured to target the character with the lowest HP, and so leaving a character in critical condition will result in another death. The spell Life 2 (or the Phoenix summon) can reduce the number of consumed turns to two, but the Revive Materia takes a long time to level up, has higher-thannormal stat penalties, and costs a lot of MP to use. Thus, the number of turns spent on reviving the victim of an instant-death attack is only reduced at significant cost, and only if the player has properly prepared for it.

3. I have adjusted for the few instances where an enemy can only cast a debuff once or can only cast it when it is the last surviving enemy in the battle.

4. I have not included the Gelnika or Ancient Forest in this analysis, as they have their own section later that explains the different rules those dungeons follow.

As you can see, the graph does not really go up steeply across the course of the game. If you plot a linear trend line for it, the r-squared value is less than 0.2. Still, there are a few things we can deduce from individual sections of the overall trend. The peak in debuffs around the Temple of the Ancients mirrors the peak in magic defense that occurs in that dungeon. Despite having seen that peak already, I expected that the use of debuffs across the whole game would increase, going from a few enemies that cast poison and slow spells to a large number of enemies who cast stop, paralyze and death. That was not the case. Instead, the difficulty in phase two of the game is mostly about inconveniencing the player with a large number of low-level debuffs rather than endangering him or her with a few higher-powered spells. The enemies in the Cave of the Gi are a good example of this. On the debuffs graph, Cosmo Canyon represents the highest point in the game up to that point, but the primary debuffs in the dungeon are poison and death sentence (which rarely takes effect in short battles). More rarely, the enemies will use paralyze, but it has a low hit rate. Poison isn't particularly deadly, but in this dungeon there are usually several enemies in a battle that can apply it, and it will eat into the party's HP. The same thing is true at the Temple of the Ancients. Enemies in this quest can apply poison, slow, sadness, darkness, frog, and berserk. (Two enemies can cast either paralyze or confuse, but do so much more rarely.) For the most part, these frequent, low-level debuffs are simply a way of lengthening battles and forcing extra effort out of the player without actually increasing the real risk of a game over.

While we're on the topic of debuffs, I want to address a common criticism of *FFVII* and the series to which it belongs. There is a long tradition of criticizing certain *FF* titles (mostly *FFIV* through *FFVII*) for filling the game with debuffs that benefit the party very little, but which benefit the enemies greatly. That is to say, when a party member attempts to inflict the silence effect, for example, the chances the spell will actually affect an enemy are quite low. This is a criticism that I think is true, but I think there is a structural reason for it. The average battle in *FFVII* should be over in about seven character turns if the characters do nothing but physically attack and never get a critical strike. Using any multi-target or enhanced-damage abilities will shorten battles even further. Even if the player were to successfully apply a debuff, that effect would barely have time to make a difference in the battle, so it's not worth wasting a turn to try. Sometimes a debuff will be useful as part of another attack through the use of the Added Effect Materia, but such a technique rarely shortens battles by much. On the other hand, enemies can apply debuffs that last longer than the battle, which extend the amount of time spent in the battle, and which significantly increase the difficulty of those battles—especially if the player doesn't have the remedy for them. Debuffs could still, in theory, be useful for the player in boss fights since the greater length of the battle would give them time to have an effect. Most of *FFVII*'s bosses are categorically immune to debuffs. Why does this need to be the case? Why couldn't debuffs work on bosses for a few rounds and then wear off? Why couldn't debuffs work against bosses but with reduced effectiveness? I can make no defense of this design decision; the designers simply missed an opportunity.

The incidence of elemental resistances follows a trend similar to debuffs, featuring a strong up-and-down motion and a nadir where one might expect a zenith. For elemental resistances, I counted the raw number of resistances appearing in a battle. Even if every enemy in a battle had the same resistance, I counted each resistance as a separate instance. I felt that this was the best way to replicate a player's experience of the game since in the early going, many players would be reliant on one or two elemental attacks like Fire 2/All or the Shiva summon. The sight of four enemies resisting damage from such a spell is thusly replicated by giving such a battle a score of four (or more, if there are other instances).[55,56]

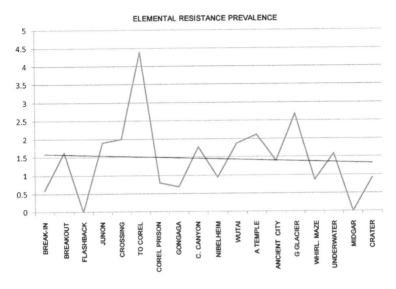

ELEMENTAL RESISTANCE PREVALENCE

Again, there is an up-and-down motion, although this time there's not as clear a peak around the Temple of the Ancients. In fact, the trend for the game is a slow, consistent drop in the prevalence of elemental resistances. The distribution of elemental resistances still reinforces the idea of phases in the game. Phase two has the most elemental resistances of any section, including the highest peak. Combine that with the relatively high magic defenses of enemies in this phase, and it's clear the designers are creating another kind of abundant (but minor) inconvenience in that phase. Aside from the extremely early peak, I was most surprised by the nadir which comes at the end of the game. I honestly expected a reasonably strong upward trend in the overall prevalence of elemental resistances, and I am thrilled to be wrong because truth is usually more interesting than prejudice.

The up-and-down structure in the incidence of elemental resistances is almost certainly another case of the designers adhering to videogame orthodoxy and varying the difficulty of sequential quests. The line bounces around a lot from the very beginning and all the way through; there are no plateaus or valleys lasting longer than two quests. The most curious feature is the extremely early peak at Mount Corel. I expect that almost nobody would name Mount Corel as the one of the tougher dungeons, and yet it has the highest average incidence of elemental resistances per battle. So what are the designers trying to accomplish there? The answer is: nothing special. Mount Corel's unusually high incidence of elemental resistances is inflated by an extremely abundant resistance to the earth element. The player could have bought the Earth Materia at Kalm, but because it costs 6000 AP to level up (whereas the Fire, Ice, and Lightning Materia require only 2000 AP each), it's not a likely candidate for use in clearing battles quickly by linking it to an All Materia. Moreover, the player has fire, ice, and wind-based summons. Why do the designers insist on an earth resistance? It's because the majority of enemies in the Mount Corel quest are birds or monsters who have traditionally hovered above the ground in previous *FF* titles. By tradition, such monsters are immune to Earth, even though Earth is a virtual non-factor in this dungeon. This is what the graph looks like with the Earth resistances removed from that quest.[57,58]

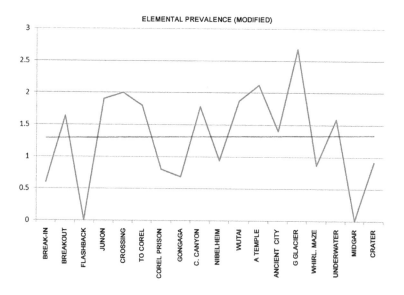

This version of the graph looks a lot more consistent across the course of the game. Obviously, that's not the true shape of the game, but it's representative of what the player experiences. Only players focusing specially on the Earth Materia are going to actually perceive the impact of the bizarre, early peak in elemental resistance.

I want to dig a little deeper in phase two to illuminate some things which the graph doesn't capture perfectly. After the early (and arbitrary) peak in elemental resistances, their prevalence decreases for a few quests before climbing again.

4. Game Difficulty and the Four Phases of *FFVII*

Elemental Resistance Prevalence in FF7 Quests

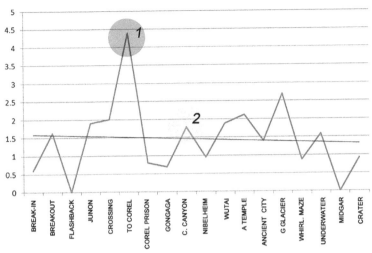

Similar to Mount Corel, the graph point representing the Cave of the Gi is propped up by resistance to one element. Almost every battle in the cave features several enemies with poison resistance. While the player certainly could be using a Bio 2/All combination, it's pretty unlikely because no enemies have been weak to the poison element by that point in the game. Still, elemental resistances are more common in that dungeon than normal. After a few more quests without much in the way of elemental resistances, Wutai and the Temple of the Ancients represent another high point. In these quests, the elemental resistances are not only plentiful but also varied. Enemies in these last two quests resist gravity, ice, fire, earth, water, and lightning in mostly equal measure. This is more in line with what we would expect from the difficulty structure of phase two: lots of small inconveniences, rising in number and diversity near the phase's final quest.

Bosses in Phase Two

Bosses are an important part of the distinction between phases as well. Phase one bosses exist to highlight basic mechanics in the game, like back attacks, counter attacks, elemental weaknesses, and debuffs. The bosses in phase two take the player on a kind of tour of the more advanced design ideas before shifting to a more damage-centric design at Nibelheim. Both parts of the phase are important, but the first part of the phase is clearly more interesting because of the different design ideas. Sample HO152 isn't terribly exciting; it casts poison and has minions and is otherwise unremarkable. The Hundred Gunner/Heli Gunner and Rufus/Dark Nation fights are much more tactically varied. The Gunners fight the party at a long range, meaning that the only way for anyone other than Barret to attack them is to cast magic or use limit breaks repeatedly. The designers are simply forcing the player to do something other than use basic attacks, and to learn about rationing their MP pool as a part of that practice. Dark Nation will cast Barrier and MBarrier on Rufus, meaning that all of Cloud's damage against him will be halved. I think it's actually quite clever of the designers that they used barriers in a fight where Cloud can't do anything about them. By forcing the player to play through a battle extended by barriers, the player gets the proper appreciation for what barriers can really do for his or her own party, and how important it is to get rid of them when the enemy has one (once this becomes possible).

Bottomswell and Jenova BIRTH are the two bosses that really stand out among the phase two lineup, but for totally different reasons. Bottomswell is unique among bosses in that it combines aspects of several earlier bosses into one. Although stacking up various challenges into one is one of the most orthodox design traditions in videogames, *FFVII* doesn't do a lot of it. Bottomswell is the exception.

 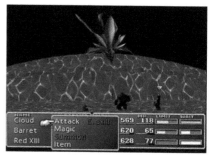

Bottomswell uses a tidal wave attack like Aps, it hovers at long range like the Gunners, and it has a prison attack like Reno. It is this last attack that is the most interesting from the perspective of traditional videogame design. Whereas Reno's prison ability simply stopped a character from acting and could be undone by physical attacks, Bottomswell's prison attack actually deals damage and can only be undone by magical attacks. Those two improvements that Bottomswell makes upon Reno's Pyramid attack are the kinds of evolutions that would not be out of place in a Mario game. Strangely enough, that kind of evolved attack doesn't appear again until phase four, and only really sees extensive use in the final battle with Sephiroth, as well as the optional fights against the Weapons. Jenova BIRTH stands out from the other bosses because she is out of phase. What I mean by this is that Jenova BIRTH has more attributes of phase three and phase four bosses than she does of other phase two bosses. In that regard, she makes for a good point of comparison for the rest of phase two. Earlier, I mentioned component stats, which are the fixed stats of a spell rather than those of a spellcaster. Because the physical and magical attack stats of enemies experience inflation across the course of the game, it's not that useful to try and compare one boss's attacks stats to another's. Component stats, however, compare quite nicely from enemy to enemy, and Jenova is unusually powerful for the section. Up until the Jenova BIRTH fight, only one boss has had an attack with a component stat of three or higher (the Air Buster). Jenova BIRTH has three attacks that powerful, one of which hits all party members, and the others of which she can use several times in a row. This would fit in perfectly well with the kind of enemies and bosses which exist in phase three, but in phase two, she's an outlier. What's more, because all of her attacks are so powerful, there's no lull in which the player can forego healing and deal extra damage. There are other bosses in the phase that can deal a lot of damage like Jenova BIRTH can, but they don't do it so consistently. The Materia Keeper casts Trine, which has a 2.125 component stat and hits all party members, but two of its other attacks only do base damage so the player has a chance to regroup in between blasts.

I think the surprising strength of Jenova BIRTH is actually a great example of consonance between the story and the gameplay. Jenova is aligned with (if not a direct manipulator of) the main antagonist of FFVII. She has unique boss music. She should be more dangerous than the average boss, and she is! Even the bosses at the Temple of the Ancients can't compare to her relative damage output. The Red Dragon and the Demons Gate have no attacks between them with a component stat of three or higher, and only one attack with a component stat higher than two. Jenova outclasses them both. But what about her second form, Jenova LIFE? She has one very powerful attack in Aqualung, which has a 3.25 component stat. Her other attacks are either equal to base damage or lower than it. I think that the reason for her relative weakness is actually story-related as well. If Jenova LIFE could wipe out the average party too easily, the player would have to watch Aeris die over and over again. That would really spoil the drama of the event, and as we have seen so many times, the FFVII development team always puts the drama first.

Phase Three: Damage Racing

Phase three of FFVII drops most of the design ideas of phase two and replaces them with a race to see who can do damage faster: the player's party or their enemies. The metaphor of a race works really well in the sense that the player's best strategy in this phase is to finish battles quickly by using high-powered, multi-target attacks. The enemy will be doing the same thing. The race metaphor fails in the sense that, although each individual battle is a race, the dungeons are about long-term attrition and the rational use of the MP pool. We've already seen how magic defense and debuffs drop off after the Temple of the Ancients; that drop-off marks the beginning of phase three. It would be a mistake, however, to imagine that this signifies a drop-off in difficulty. Actually, enemies in phase three are a threat to the player for the first time. Most of this increased threat comes in the form of powered-up special attacks. Special attacks are unique enemy techniques like "Claw," "Tentacle," and "Extreme Bomber," which the player never learns. These attacks are governed by component stats that rise markedly in this phase. Equally important, however, are the abilities that player characters gain. Increasing amounts of AP make it so that magic and support materia are more powerful, and the player can cast high-level magic against multiple targets several times per battle. Beyond that, players also have lots of powerful summons, several of which deal non-elemental damage. The designers put these abilities in the game specifically for the player to use them in normal battles, and phase three gives the player a good incentive to do so.

Scaling Simple Damage

Even from the earliest days of the RPG, there have been unnecessarily complicated damage and hit formulas. Anyone who played *D&D* in the days of THAC0 (to hit armor class zero) can attest to that. The primary formula for damage in *FFVII* is fairly complex as well. Several times already, I've spoken about the how component stat was useful for tracking enemy damage output across the game. It's important, however, to understand why that's the case. Below is the two-step formula for determining physical damage.

$$\text{Base Damage} = \text{Att} + [(\text{Att} + \text{Lvl})/32] * [(\text{Att} * \text{Lvl})/32] \quad (4.1)$$

$$\text{Actual Damage} = [(\text{Power} * (512 - \text{Def}) * \text{Base Damage})/(16 * 512)] \quad (4.2)$$

We've already seen that enemy attack stats and player defense stats (and vice versa) rise in step with each other across the course of the game. That is, the designer has a set of guidelines for how high a monster's attack stat can be in a given quest. The same is true for enemy levels. Enemies can only be one or two levels higher in the Great Glacier than they were in the City of the Ancients or else the player will have to spend several hours grinding between quests. (There's a place for grinding in *FF* titles, but it's not in the mid-game.) The only part of the formula which isn't limited to a fixed range by quest is the "power" variable, which is the component stat I discussed earlier. The component stat for enemy attacks is the place where the designers effectively determine damage-based difficulty for each quest.

Looking at the value of component stats across the course of the game tells us a lot about enemy design and the overall difficulty structure of *FFVII*. Like everything else in the game, the value of component stats goes up and down. The graph below visualizes the value of component stats across the course of the game, on a per-battle basis.[59,60]

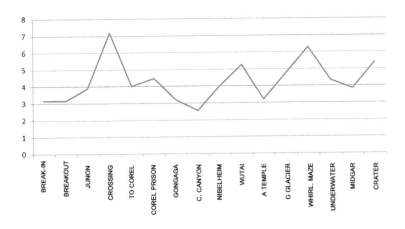

AVERAGE COMPONENT STAT OF MOST POWERFUL ABILITY PER QUEST

Many enemies have more than one ability that has a component stat, and so for this graph I have only visualized the highest-damage ability for each enemy in a battle. I have also adjusted the value to reflect not just the value of the component stat, but also the number of targets that the attack can hit. On top of that, I added together the highest damage attack for each enemy in a battle as a representation of the total top-end enemy power available in that battle. Finally, I charted the average of all the battles in each quest on that basis. This isn't a perfect representation of how each battle will proceed since an enemy might not use their most powerful attack every time, but it does give a good idea of how much damage a given battle will dish out relative to other battles and other quests.

One point on the graph is a red herring that needs further explanation. The quest with the greatest damage output from random enemies in the entire game is, apparently, the crossing from Junon to Costa del Sol. I doubt very much that anyone who has actually played the game thinks this is accurate, and in a certain sense, they're right. The data point is unusually high because the Marine enemy, which appears in every battle, has an attack that hits all party members for moderately elevated damage. Because these enemies appear in every battle in that dungeon, they pull the average component stat up significantly. The reason why nobody thinks of this as the hardest quest is that there are only two rooms with random encounters inside the belly of the cargo ship. Even players who explore every inch of the ship's interior will only run into half a dozen encounters. While the component stats for this section of the game are unusually high, the dungeon is too brief to be much of a threat. The data are skewed by a very small sample size. If we remove that unusual quest, we are left with a graph that tells a clearer story.

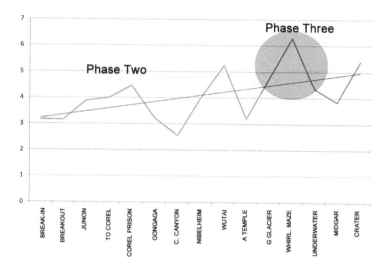

The last thing I want to do is to alter the data so that they reinforce my thesis, but there are a few good reasons for visualizing the data this way. Firstly, there is only one major exception to the low/moderate component stats that are found in phase two. If there were three quests that broke the pattern, there would be no pattern, but one exception does not negate the larger rule. Secondly, one of the things we have seen again and again in this book (and will continue to see) is that the designers of *FFVII* put the storytelling aspects of their game ahead of everything else. The cargo ship's small size (relative to other dungeons) is a product of that. The designers could send the player through all the ducts of the cargo ship, fighting a variety of enemies along the way, but that doesn't happen. That wouldn't fit the fiction of the quest (i.e., the size of the ship), and that fiction is the most important part of the game. Thus, we get a smaller sample size of enemy attacks which affects the shape of the unaltered graph.

There are four other points on the graph that explain the philosophy behind enemy ability design in *FFVII*. The first two I want to examine are the Great Glacier and Gaea's Cliffs/Whirlwind Maze quests, which form the heart of phase three. Both quests are filled with enemies with strong attacks like the Headbomber's ability Extreme Bomber, which has a 4.375 component stat, and the Lessaploth's Avalanche, which has a 3.75 component stat and targets all party members. These enemies appear often and in normal quantities, meaning that players have to make an important choice: do they spend MP to kill these enemies quickly or do they spend MP to heal after taking several rounds of damage? One way or another, the player is going to have to spend MP. Unlike the Cargo Ship dungeon, the Great Glacier and Gaea's Cliffs/Whirlwind Maze dungeons are quite long. The Great Glacier consists of 12 large maps and lots of generic connecting maps which make it difficult to navigate. It's the one dungeon where the player might really get lost.

It's easy for players to get lost in the many similar-looking sections of the glacier and for their party to become depleted of MP and items, no matter what strategy they use. Eventually, the party will faint and wake up at Holzoff's house, but the quest can really drag on and endanger unprepared players. Based on the data collected about the design, it seems like the designers intended for the player to use big attacks rather than spend MP healing in this phase. Below I have visualized the changeover from using the strongest available multi-target summon (Titan) in the final four quests in phase two, and then the same thing (but for Bahamut) in the first four quests for phase three. In each quest, the damage is calculated using the average magic defense enemies have in that quest.[61]

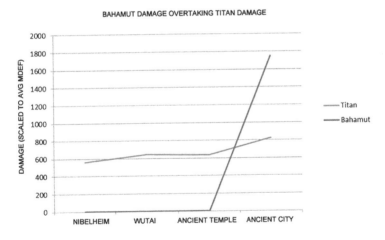

The difference is stark. Not only is Bahamut way more powerful than Titan, but the lower magic defenses of the enemies in the post-Bahamut quests makes the difference in damage even more pronounced. This trend continues throughout phase three. In the graph below, the blue line is the damage from the highest available summon, while the red line is average enemy HP for the phase three quests. In phase three, the player gains the ability to wipe out a battle with a single summon, whereas in most of phase two that only works in a few battles.[62]

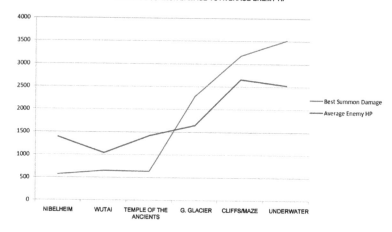

AVERAGE SUMMON DAMAGE VS AVERAGE ENEMY HP

The player's ability to blow through battles isn't limited to just non-elemental summons like Bahamut or summons at all; non-summon elemental spells are still totally in play. We saw earlier how elemental resistances drop across the course of the game, but I want to examine the elemental resistances in phase three because they highlight the change in player spellcasting. To that end, I'm going to bring back the elemental resistances graph with another highlight.

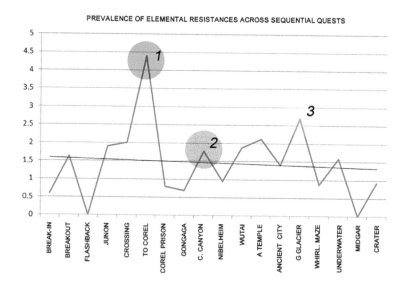

PREVALENCE OF ELEMENTAL RESISTANCES ACROSS SEQUENTIAL QUESTS

There's a slight uptick in the prevalence of resistances in the Great Glacier quest, but afterwards elemental resistances drop significantly. (The uptick in Great Glacier is mostly just in one element: nearly every enemy is strong against ice,

4. Game Difficulty and the Four Phases of *FFVII*

but all the other elements are viable.) At first glance, this drop-off seems strange, but it's probably deliberate. Designers might round up on the amount of EXP an enemy provides, and they might be careless with the occasional magic stat, but game-wide elemental resistances are not such a casual affair. I think that the reason that the designers chose to use a progressively smaller number of elemental resistances is that it allows the player to use a greater variety of attacks. What's the point of putting all that time and energy into leveling up the Lightning and Leviathan Materia if they are progressively less useful as elemental resistances become more prevalent? This would make it impossible to blow through battles in one or two attacks, which is the essence of phase three.

The reduction in the prevalence of elemental resistances is actually a good example of how the materia system in *FFVII* separates it structurally from other entries in the series. In *FFV* or *FFVI*, it's easy to teach a character several different kinds of elemental and non-elemental attacks. There's also no limit to the size of a character's spell book in those games; given enough time, every character can learn every spell. Except for having to invest time, there's no drawback to learning a wide range of spells. In *FFVII*, where an elemental spell fills one of the limited number of materia slots and each materia penalizes the player's stats, it's not really possible for every character to have access to every spell. Thus, it's all too easy to go into a battle in *FFVII* without having the appropriate elemental spell available on more than one character. In that light, the late-game reduction in elemental resistances makes sense; players would be irritated to find that the 45,000 AP they have gained in their favorite materia is a wasted effort because so many enemies are immune.

Bosses in Phase Three

Bosses in phase three are less interesting from a mechanical perspective than they are from a statistical perspective. The only boss in phase three which does something really interesting mechanically is the Carry Armor, which shows us another evolution of the idea of imprisoned party members. All the other bosses in the phase are built around some version of statistical brute force. Still, sometimes the designers still manage to do something clever in that regard. A couple of bosses (including the Carry Armor, again) have multiple parts that put out significant damage. Multi-part bosses are not new in the third phase. Sample HO512 and Gi Nattak both had minions; they just didn't do that much damage. By contrast, the multiple parts of Schizo and Carry Armor deal damage far in excess of what their base stats would suggest. There are also some quasi-bosses on the train bound for North Corel which subvert the player's expectations of what to do in a phase-three battle just by being unusually durable. All of the bosses, however, tend to eschew debuffs in favor of throwing out large amounts of damage in a fairly straightforward fashion.

One of the odd things about bosses in phase three is that the component stats of their attacks aren't higher than those of bosses in phase two. This doesn't mean that these bosses can't output more damage than their predecessors; they just have to do it in a different way. Below I have visualized the average of each boss's component stat across the course of phases two and three.[63]

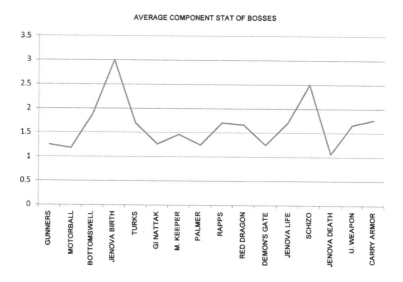

AVERAGE COMPONENT STAT OF BOSSES

For random enemies in phases two and three, I visualized the component stat of each monster's most powerful attack, whereas in this graph, I visualized the average of a boss's attacks. My reasoning for this is that boss battles last long enough for the boss to use all their abilities more or less equally (and their behavior scripts virtually guarantee that they will do so). Thus, the player's experience of a boss's damage output is, I think, closer to the average of its attacks than to its highest attack. In any case, I'm comparing bosses to other bosses here, so the difference between them and common enemies is mostly irrelevant. The graph can be deceptive because bosses—especially those in phase three—aren't perfectly represented by their stats. Jenova DEATH, in particular, has bafflingly low component stats to her attacks. She's a great example of what's going on in boss design in phase three, however. Jenova DEATH can use her "Red Light" attack three times in a row—and frequently does. Non-boss enemies can use two attacks in a row, but they usually intersperse these double attacks with a single action. Jenova DEATH always attacks twice in a row when she uses Red Light, and frequently attacks three times in a row. Similarly, both of Schizo's heads can attack in sequence and all three parts of the Carry Armor can cause damage in one turn. While these bosses aren't equipped with especially high component stats, they can deal damage as though they were.

     4. Game Difficulty and the Four Phases of *FFVII*

Phase three also features the closest thing this game has to mid- or mini-bosses, in the quest to retrieve the huge materia from North Corel. Each of the enemies on the materia train is unique to the quest and has an unusually high amount of HP, especially the Wolfmeister and Eagle Gun. Both of these enemies have HP on par with those in the monsters of the Northern Crater. On the other hand, neither monster does that much damage. The role of these enemies is to subvert the player's normal phase-three strategy. Phase three calls for the player to use high-powered attacks to get through battles before the enemy can deal too much damage to the party. Many of these powerful attacks—especially summons— have long animations which will eat up the timer that is ticking down during this quest. Thus, players who have been relying on summons or other spells with long animations will actually hurt their own chances of completing the quest successfully and getting the full rewards. This inversion of expectation is one of the oldest design tropes in videogames, going back all the way to the early Mario games. Although this is one of the only instances of such an inversion in the game, it does show some evidence of the influence of action games on the RPG in its digital form.

Phase Four

As we saw in Chapter 1 of this book, the kind of RPG that the *Final Fantasy* team wanted to make could not include the tactical elements that had been essential to the RPG formula from the very beginning. *Final Fantasy VI* took the first step towards a class-agnostic system by using armor, stat, and magic systems that gave no particular class an advantage over any other. *Final Fantasy VII* consummated this trend by tactically denuding its characters, except for Aeris. The second-greatest mistake that critics make about *FFVII* is in thinking that nothing filled the void left by tactics. The complexity is delivered via the level-up system, which becomes more intricate in phase four. Essentially, the designers move the complexity out of the individual battle and into the long-term preparation for and recovery from that battle. To explain how this happened, I'm going to talk first

---

about how the fourth phase of *FFVII* presents a new kind of difficulty, and then how the endgame content solves that difficulty.

In phase four, changes to the structure of the level-up system force the player to become more resourceful. The most obvious change is in the jumps in monster levels between dungeons. For most of the game, the player enters a quest either at the appropriate level or slightly above or below it. In phase four, the player's party usually enters a quest at a level beneath that of the enemies. The chart below describes the median level (based on appearances in actual encounters rather than a bestiary list) of enemies in quests throughout the game.[64]

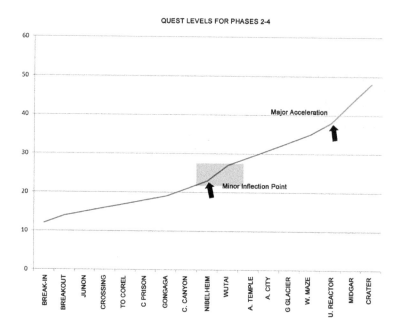

To some degree, this is just supposed to make the dungeons harder, and it does. First, there is a small jump in the level of enemies in the Return to Midgar quest, and then there is a larger jump in enemy levels in the Northern Crater. Those jumps are the marker which makes phase four distinct.

It would be easy to see the bigger gaps in median enemy level as the worst kind of RPG difficulty. One of the things that free-to-play/freemium games revealed in RPG systems is the problem of boring stat inflation. Games that are trying to incentivize in-app purchases will use a variety of tactics to make their games almost unplayable so that the player will spend money. One strategy for this is to make each character level require a quadratically, or exponentially, higher amount of EXP points to reach. *Final Fantasy VII* does not do this; in fact, the number of battles required to gain a level actually goes down markedly toward the end of the game. Of course, requiring the player to level up three times in a quest instead of

4. Game Difficulty and the Four Phases of *FFVII*

once is similar to making the gap between levels wider. So *FFVII* could be said to achieve the same effect through different means, although I'll explain why I don't think that's the case here. The short version is that although the gap in levels grows steeply, this is actually a kind of puzzle for which the game provides several pieces. Another strategy that F2P games frequently use to incentivize purchases is sudden leaps in enemy stats, regardless of level. We've already seen that this isn't true for *FFVII*. Enemies in the fourth phase have medium stats, medium debuffs, medium component stats, and low elemental resistances. It is through the sum of these statistical increases, plus the larger gaps in levels between quests/dungeons, that *FFVII's* last phase gets its difficulty.

As in the discussion of the first three phases, I want to highlight some of the finer details that don't appear in large-scale statistical analysis. There are some unusual methods in enemy design in phase four, especially in the Northern Crater. (Although they are a part of phase four, I leave the discussion of the Gelnika and Ancient Forest for their own section.) The first new idea to enter enemy design is an increase in the prevalence of instantly lethal abilities. In the earlier analyses of the prevalence of debuffs, I said that I expected the worst debuffs like death, stop, paralyze, and petrify to appear more frequently at the end of the game, and they do. Death spells, in particular, are much more common on enemies in the Northern Crater than in any other place. (Other debuffs make a moderate comeback, too.) It doesn't take a direct death spell for enemies in the Northern Crater to kill a party member. Several enemies in the final dungeon have other abilities that deal so much damage that they will kill either one or several party members. The best example of this is the Allemagne's Level 3 Flare, which has a damage modifier set to 120% of the target's HP, meaning instant death if not mitigated by another effect. Similarly, the Dark Dragon can cast Ultima, the strongest spell in the game available to a non-boss monster, and the King Behemoth will cast Comet 2. In each case, these highly-damaging spells are only used as a counterattack against magical abilities the player uses. The Dark Dragon and the Allemagne will also only use their best attack once per battle, as do several other slightly less-threatening enemies like the Scissors.

With one exception, the attacks listed above aren't really meant to kill an entire party at once because *FFVII* just isn't that kind of game. Only one ability in the entire dungeon is meant to cause a game over, and that belongs to the Dark Dragon. The Dark Dragon appears in the first section of the final dungeon, and its Ultima spell will probably wipe out parties below level 50, or those that aren't using high magic-defense gear like the Zeidreich or Aegis Armlet or protective spells like Mbarrier or Big Guard. In that sense, the Dark Dragon serves as a great spot-check to tell the player whether his or her party is ready for the Northern Crater at all. The best answer that a first-time player can really receive is "no," because there is a lot to do and see outside of the final dungeon. The other non-boss enemies tend to kill party members one at a time or weaken the whole party by a moderate amount. This change reflects an evolution of the design ideas from phase three. It's still in the player's best interest to end battles quickly because the enemies in phase four are deadly in many different ways. It's just that in phase four, the player can't plow through battles with summons and high-powered magic as he could in phase three. Not only are magic defenses back up to moderate levels, but many of the enemies will save their best spells for counterattacks against magic. Essentially, many enemies in the final dungeon have become like the first boss, but without the obvious warning of the raised tail.

The other way in which phase four evolves the primary dynamic of phase three is by deploying enemies and battles that cannot be rushed through by any means. Although the player continues to acquire powerful summons and other magic throughout the game, some enemies are virtually guaranteed to get off several attacks before dying. Sometimes this is through obvious means; the Dark Dragon, Iron Man, Dragon Zombie, and especially Master Tonberry cannot be easily defeated in one or two turns because they have some combination of high HP, high magic defenses, and elemental resistances. Even with attacks like 4x-Cut or some of the later limit breaks, these enemies will probably still get off between two and five attacks, many of which are highly damaging. Other enemies, like the Gargoyle, are guaranteed an attack by a combination of temporary invulnerability and counterattacking behaviors. The result of this is that players—especially those with under-levelled characters—have to both spend MP to get through battles quickly and spend MP to recover afterwards. With only one save point available in the entire final dungeon, there's no reliably cheap way to restore those MP. Thus, the player is going to have to be careful about resource management in this dungeon in a way they haven't ever been before.

Rationing and Attrition

More than half of what phase four has to offer is located outside the final dungeon, and because of that, I have given that content its own section. Before getting to that, however, I want to talk about how the final dungeon is supposed to help the player understand how the rest of phase four works. In *FFVII*, as is the case in most of the *FF* titles up to this point, MP are not cheap. The purchasable item that restores MP in *FFVII* is the Ether, which grants 100 MP for the price of 1500 gil. This isn't terribly expensive as far as items in *FFVII* go, but it's not trivial. Battles in the Northern Crater drop an average of 2,600 gil. To look at it another way, the party earns about 400 gil per basic physical attack, on average, in the Northern Crater. (Actually, both of these averages discount the Mover enemy, which dispenses tons of gil but appears so rarely that it doesn't affect the overall rate much.) At that rate of return, the cost of Ethers will seriously cut into the player's gil earnings, and that has real drawbacks which we'll discuss below. The player has to figure out some other strategy for getting through the dungeon with a fresh party and a good stockpile of items for the three sequential last bosses.

There are several ways around the price of MP, but those methods (mostly) force the player to engage in activities other than grinding in the final dungeon. The most obvious way that the player can mitigate the cost of MP is by stealing

4. Game Difficulty and the Four Phases of *FFVII*

MP from enemies. I wrote extensively about MP management and dungeon attrition in *Reverse Design: Final Fantasy VI*, and many readers made the totally justified criticism that everything I wrote was moot because the Osmose spell was incredibly effective at stealing MP from virtually any target. I can offer no comprehensive defense against that criticism. I don't know whether the part of the *FFVI* design team in charge of dungeons failed to communicate with the part of the team in charge of spell design or whether it was a deliberate decision. Whatever they intended for *FFVI*, the ability to steal MP in *FFVII* is significantly reduced. The MP Absorb Materia makes a nice pair with a number of other attacks, but it's a unique item, it only absorbs 1% of damage dealt as MP, and it takes 100,000 AP to master it. If the player wants to spread the ability to steal MP around to more than one character, they'll have to be clever about power-leveling the materia. As we'll see in Chapter 5, specifically targeting certain materia for power-leveling is one of the things that the designers wanted the player to do, but that doesn't mean MP are cheap and abundant—especially not in long dungeons.

The player can also cheat. In every *Reverse Design*, I try to make a point of writing about the game that actually exists, rather than the game that the designers wanted to make. For *FFVI*, this meant I had to acknowledge the legendary Vanish/Doom trick, and the fact that the evade stat doesn't do anything. There's a big difference between the Vanish/Doom exploit in *FFVI* and the W-Item duplication trick in *FFVII*. When the player uses Vanish and Doom to instantly kill a boss in *FFVI*, those spells are working exactly as intended. Obviously, the designers did not foresee the power of this combination, but there weren't any programming errors involved. Moreover, most of the toughest bosses are totally immune to this combination, so the game still presents a challenge. In *FFVII*, the player can take advantage of a programming error to duplicate items (like megalixirs) with the W-Item Materia, thereby totally bypassing any concerns about gil or MP rationing. It would be wrong of me not to address the reality of this, but at the same time, I think the W-Item trick is philosophically different from the Vanish/Doom trick. The former is a bug, the latter is an emergent strategy. Beyond that, I know from firsthand experience that many players did not even obtain the W-Item Materia on their first few trips through *FFVII*. Even though the W-Item trick obviates much of the analysis to come, I'm going to continue with it because it reflects the experience of those who played without exploiting that bug (deliberately or in ignorance), and those who continue to do so even to this day on platforms for which the bug was repaired.

The most important way to mitigate the struggle to ration MP in the final dungeon is to collect the numerous powerful weapons, items, and materia that exist outside of it. In phase three, the player gains numerous new attacks, but virtually all of them are in the form of MP-expensive materia. In phase four, the player has the time and resources to obtain powerful command materia like 2x-Cut, Mime, and Counter. There are also powerful weapons, many of which don't require any dungeon crawling at all, like the Ultima Weapon, Venus Gospel, Death Penalty, Limited Moon, and Final Heart. There is a summon materia so powerful that its high MP cost doesn't even matter because it ends virtually any battle in one or two casts. There are also materia and equips that enhance the rate of EXP and AP gain. Essentially, there's an entire peripheral level-up system that exists in phase four that does not require the player's party to be at a high character level. (Technically, some of these things can either be obtained at the end of phase three or the process to obtain them can be started then, but for most of them it's much easier to simply start in phase four.) It is by exploring these other options that the player will encounter the rich complexity that FFVII has to offer. But the peripheral level-up system—or what I like to call "wide levels"—is so deep that it requires its own section, which follows the discussion of phase four bosses.

Bosses in Phase Four

Battles with bosses in phase four become longer, but not always more difficult. Below is a graph of boss HP across the course of the game, which increases far more than any other stat a boss has.[65]

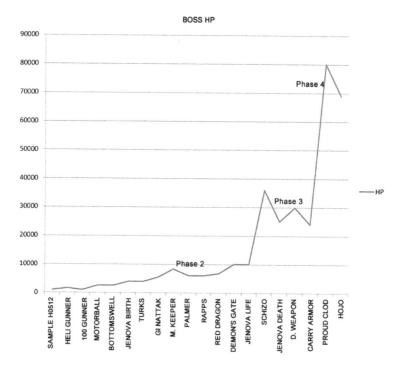

There is an explosion in boss HP in phase four. The important things to notice about this explosion is how sudden it is, and how it's so much larger than the previous increase (which happened right before the beginning of phase three). The interesting thing here is that HP is the only stat that goes up so sharply. Magic defense, for example, doesn't go up consistently across the course of the game, as you can see below.

Boss attack stats (not pictured) do go up, but they only do so in the same way that all attack stats go up—the growth is not explosive. Boss component stats don't really inflate at all. None of Diamond Weapon, the Turks, the Proud Clod, or Jenova SYNTHESIS regularly uses an attack with a component stat above three. Diamond Weapon has a fraction attack that depletes party health to 1/8, but this is preceded by a long countdown and succeeded by a brief cooldown. Similarly, Jenova SYNTHESIS will cast Ultima after a long and obvious cooldown, giving the player lots of time to prepare for the blast. For the most part, the boss fights in phase four are just longer, not harder. The two exceptions to this are Hojo and Safer Sephiroth, but I'll address their more powerful (and frequent) attacks individually after talking about the HP explosion.

Two factors account for the increase in boss HP: the caster's advantage and the introduction of wide levels. The caster's advantage is a design dynamic that arises from the scaling of spell effects when MP costs are fixed. That is, the Fire 2 spell gets stronger as the character casting it gains levels, stats and new equipment. The MP cost for Fire 2 remains at 22 forever. Thus, the damage output of a character's MP pool grows like this for a single spell:[66,67]

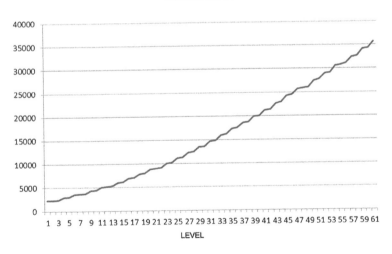

TOTAL DAMAGE UNTIL MP DEPLETION USING SECOND-LEVEL ELEMENTAL SPELL

Because bosses are always preceded by save points and because MP can be restored to full at a save point, players never have to ration their characters' MP during a boss fight. The caster's advantage makes that strategy even more effective as the game goes on. There is a drawback in the need for healing spells, however. The player's pool of HP grows along with the boss's ability to do damage. That is, although the player characters are always growing into a higher maximum

HP, the boss's ability to reduce that HP grows commensurately. Thus, the caster's advantage is not as advantageous when it comes to healing.[67,68]

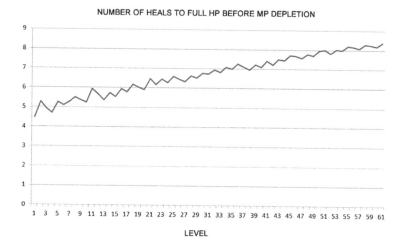

NUMBER OF HEALS TO FULL HP BEFORE MP DEPLETION

LEVEL

Although the amount of healing per MP spent grows, the need for healing grows so much that the caster does not enjoy as comfortable a margin as in the case of attack magic. Much of the MP spent during a boss fight will be on recovery, cutting even further into the marginal gains from the caster's advantage on the damage side of the equation. There is another factor driving up boss HP that supplements the gains from the caster's advantage.

The other component driving up boss HP is the implementation of wide levels. Chapter 5 covers that topic, but I want to give an illustration of the idea. Sephiroth is the only boss in the game whose HP and stats scale up in a really noticeable way, as long as the player characters meet certain criteria. For every party member at level 99, Safer Sephiroth gains an additional 80,000 HP,[69] which is equal to his base HP. All of his character stats also climb markedly. In spite of this increase in stats, players who get every one of their party members to level 99 invariably obliterate Safer Sephiroth in a few turns. Along the way to level 99, the player has collected so many items and leveled up their materia so many times that it doesn't matter if Sephiroth climbs to level 99 with them. When equipped with the best weapons, the best materia and using the best items, the player's party doesn't just climb to level 99—it's more like they're using characters who are effectively at level 150 or 200. That power, and the path to acquiring it, are the place where *FFVII*'s design gets really interesting.

Hojo and Sephiroth both benefit from this explosion in HP, but they also have other factors that make them dangerous. Hojo uses debuffs often: he will routinely inflict poison, confuse, sleep, and silence. His real strength, though, is that his basic physical attack Pile Banger has a 3.125 component stat, which is high for a basic attack. Hojo's third form, meanwhile, actually combines the numerous debuffs with a strong physical attack. The third form's Combo attack has a total component stat of 2.187, but it also inflicts poison, darkness, and sleep on its target along with all that damage. For most bosses, the extra HP doesn't do anything except make the fight longer. In the battle with Hojo, the extra length gives all those debuffs a chance to eat up lots of player turns. By contrast, the fight against the Proud Clod is long just for the sake of being dramatic, much like the Black Tyrano fight in *Chrono Trigger*. The Hojo fight is both long and dangerous.

Sephiroth, especially in his second form, does everything that Hojo does, but to a more extreme extent. Sephiroth's first "Bizarro" form relies mostly on magic, including third-level elemental spells that have component stats of four to 4.375. His debuff attack, Stigma, has a 1.375 component stat (backed by a high physical attack stat) and applies poison and slow. He also uses multi-target fraction attacks, including a unique one that reduces all party members to one HP. The real cornerstone of the Bizarro form, however, is Sephiroth's ability to heal himself. Although a properly-prepared party will have no problem dealing more damage than Sephiroth can heal, players whose parties are too low in level can easily become demoralized by his regeneration. This is especially true of players that have to consume too many turns healing their own party. Overall, though, only the fraction attacks are a real threat to knock out the player's party.

Safer Sephiroth is considerably more deadly, as he possesses all the most dangerous types of attacks the game employs. Even his physical attack is dangerous; although the component stat for this attack is only 1.5, it inflicts paralyze and darkness. His weakest single-target magical attack has a 3.18 component stat and inflicts sadness, frog, and small. His strongest magic attack (the legendary Supernova) hits all party members for 93% of their health, and inflicts confusion, silence and slow. He has two other magical attacks with component stats above six. What separates Safer Sephiroth from all the other story bosses is that he has no attack that constitutes a lull. Jenova SYNTHESIS has a variety of powerful attacks, but there are points in the battle during which she's counting down to Ultima, and in that moment the player has a little extra time to heal, apply buffs, or deal extra damage. In the Safer Sephiroth fight, there's no such time; Sephiroth seriously hurts at least one party member per turn. Thus, at least one character usually needs to be healing and cleansing debuffs all the time. Earlier, I weighted the distribution of debuffs based on the number of character turns those debuffs would consume. Sephiroth's constant use of debuffs in this battle certainly consumes some turns, but so does his constant damage output. A player who is spending turns removing debuffs and healing cannot attack. Thus, the length of the final battle is extended, not by a gratuitously large HP pool, as in the case of many phase four bosses, but by an endless series of deadly attacks.

Optional Bosses

The optional bosses Ultimate, Emerald and Ruby Weapon all follow the Sephiroth template to some degree. Ultimate Weapon is the easiest of the three, but it still employs one part of the formula that makes Sephiroth dangerous. All of Ultimate Weapon's attacks are damaging enough that the player has to dedicate a party member to healing at least every other turn. Its weakest attack is a spell with a component stat of 1.5 that hits every party member. It doesn't use many debuffs, but all of its attacks are above base damage and most of them can hit more than one party member at a time.

Emerald Weapon is the best example of pure brute force in *FFVII*. Obviously, it has incredibly high base stats, although we've seen many times how those aren't the most meaningful indicator of difficulty. That said, Emerald Weapon's component stats absolutely back up its statistical underpinnings. The monster's most-used attack has a component stat of 5.6, while two of its regenerating minions have a primary attack with a component stat of 6.9.[70] Although Emerald Weapon does not use debuffs, nearly all of its abilities remove party member buffs like regen, mbarrier, and haste.[71] Because of the huge amounts of damage that it and its minions can put out, players can easily lose turns to Emerald Weapon while trying to constantly heal and re-apply buffs—even more so than in the Sephiroth fight.

The closest thing to fighting a powered-up version of Sephiroth is fighting Ruby Weapon. Like Emerald Weapon, it deals tons of damage, but it also uses debuffs and has a nasty gimmick attack. Ruby Weapon's most prominent attack has a component stat of 6.25,[72] hits the entire party, and inflicts paralysis. It also has a spell with a component stat of 3 that inflicts confusion, and four attacks which cut a party member's HP by a set fraction and inflict frog, small, poison and slow. The difficult thing about the Sephiroth fight is the lack of a lull; the player can easily get behind in the damage department while spending turns healing. If the loss of character turns is dangerous, however, then Ruby Weapon has the deadliest weapon in the game: he can remove up to two party members from the battle entirely. This is the final evolution of the design idea that began in the first fight with Reno. Reno imprisoned party members in a pyramid that could be cleared by physical attacks. In the Bottomswell fight, that prison attack became a bubble that dealt damage and was only vulnerable to magic. The Carry Armor is able to imprison two enemies until its arms are destroyed. Ruby Weapon can knock two party members out of the battle entirely—an attack that the player cannot do anything to cure. Although the AI of Ruby Weapon can be exploited to avoid this ability, most players on their first trip through the game aren't going to figure that out. This leaves the player with one party member who has to both heal and deal damage. That—in this author's view—is the absolute peak of the challenges in *FFVII*.

Finding Complexity in Wide Levels

A large portion of the content in phase four exists outside of the mandatory dungeons. The purpose of this content is to allow the player to build his or her party's power through means other than repeating the same few battles in the final dungeon over and over again. Earlier, I talked about the concept of "wide levels." To explain what this term means, it's necessary to provide some context to how we think about level-based progression systems in RPGs. Since the days of *D&D*, a level-up has always been a permanent, periodic increase in character power. The most obvious example of this is when a character goes from being level 23 to level 24. That's a permanent condition; it happens at regular intervals as measured by experience, and it's an increase in power. Several other events fit the same criteria, however. An obvious example of this is the levels gained by materia, which go from casting simple spells to more powerful spells, or which allow the player to cast a summon spell multiple times per battle as they grow in level. Equipment is also a form of level-up. The growth from level 23 to level 24 is qualitatively the same as the growth from the Titan Bangle to the Mithril Bangle. Gear may not seem as permanent as character levels because players often sell it, but they only sell their old gear when they have access to a new and better piece of gear. Players can't "sell" level 23 when they reach 24, but they would if they could. Sold or not, gear is just another level-up system that offers permanent periodic increases in player power.

If levels can take many different forms, we can assess level-up systems in terms of height and width. The height of a level up system is easy to measure; it's simply the number of increments between the player's starting level and the maximum. For *FFVII*, the character level system goes from four to 99 (no character starts below level four), for a height of 96 increments. That's fairly tall, although many JRPGs have passed it since. There are lots of other heights to measure, though. Cloud has 16 weapons to collect, each one a level-up. Every character has seven limit breaks to learn, each one a level-up. If we're looking for width, we're looking to see how many different systems contribute permanently to character power. My count is five different systems: character levels, limit break levels, materia levels, equipment levels, and chocobo levels. It's not immediately obvious how chocobo levels affect character power, but we'll get to that later. The important thing to realize is that there are many different systems that strengthen the player's characters.

There's more to the design of a wide level-up system than merely having different bars to fill. For width to actually work as a design philosophy, the player has to engage in different kinds of activities to fill those bars or else the player is only grinding. Most of the above systems are based on battles, but not all of them. The best materia and gear are both acquired through various kinds of exploration. Although players certainly can become powerful enough to beat Sephiroth and the optional bosses through mere grinding, it actually takes less time (and fewer repetitions) to pursue non-battle tasks in conjunction with some grinding, rather than grinding until the character level cap is reached.

The point of wide levels is to reintroduce complexity that was stripped from battles when character classes disappeared. The really brilliant thing about *FFVII's* level-up system is not that it's just wide, but that all of its diverse systems interact with one another in different ways, giving clever players a way of manipulating all of these systems to their party's advantage. All of the different level-up systems run on different currencies, and these currencies come at different rates. What's more, those rates change over time. The primary example of this dynamic is the change in the ratio of EXP to both gil and AP.[73,74]

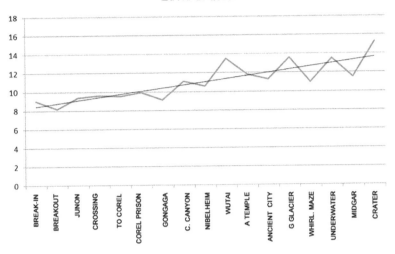

EXP: AP BY QUEST

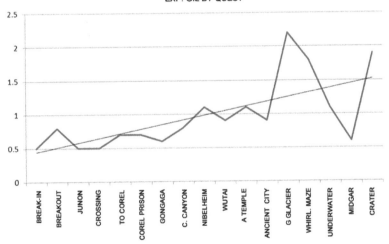

EXP: GIL BY QUEST

One explanation for this dynamic is that the characters' EXP needs grow more than their AP needs grow, and the total amount of EXP needed is vastly larger. But this doesn't explain how the player is supposed to grow materia like Ultima, Contain, Bahamut Zero, and Knights of the Round. All of these materia arrive late in the game, start at zero AP growth, and have huge AP requirements, all without a commensurate increase in AP income. The designers aren't simply making a mistake here, however; the game is changing to give the player new ways to play the game.

Before players have even thought about the major sidequests, they are met with a puzzle that comes out of the phase four level system. The difference in currency rates has had two important results already: the player has a gil surplus and an AP deficit. The ratio of gil to EXP has actually gone down, but because the player no longer has to purchase gear, they will start to accumulate it in the endgame phase. An accumulation of money at the end of a JRPG is a fairly common occurrence, and different games have dealt with the surplus differently. *Star Ocean: The Second Story* features a shop in the middle of its optional dungeon whose contents are so expensive (although they are worth the money) that players can never expect to buy them all. *Final Fantasy VIII* employed an item transmutation system that allowed players to turn certain common, purchasable items into more powerful items or even directly into magic, thereby putting excess money to use. *Final Fantasy VII* also takes advantage of the surplus by allowing the player to invest that money into chocobo breeding. Neither *Star Ocean* nor *FFVIII* has anything like the AP deficit that exists in *FFVII*, however. (*Star Ocean's* ability points system is folded into its level-ups, while *FFVIII's* ability points are actually much easier to farm than EXP is if the player knows where to do it.) The ideal solution to the surplus/deficit problem would be to turn gil into EXP, and by complicated means, this is actually possible.

EXP Alchemy

The signature cycle which drives the end-game content in *FFVII* is the transformation of excess gil into EXP and AP. The means of this transformation is through the Gold Saucer, primarily via chocobo racing. Because the player no longer needs to buy gear, he or she can invest their excess gil into something other than equipment purchases. One strategy would be to simply invest it all in purchasing Ethers, which would allow for the replenishment of MP while in a dungeon. This strategy will work, but it's not efficient and requires nonstop grinding. Although the upfront costs for chocobo breeding are high and the payoff is not immediately visible, it's still the best investment in the game.

5. Finding Complexity in Wide Levels

For players who are not duplicating items, the cost of chocobo greens, stalls, and nuts can accumulate quickly. The rewards, although not immediate, are extremely good. To the right is a table of items that can be won from races. The items here are a mixed bag. Some of them are useless trash and some are useful, but not worth doing races for. Some of them, however, are incredibly valuable. Materia like Enemy Away and Counter Attack have clear uses, but it's the elixir item that holds the most value. Elixirs can be converted into large amounts of EXP (and decent amounts of AP) through the Magic Pot monster.

The Magic Pot can be found in the Northern Crater (its exact position and encounter rate are discussed later.) After being doused with an Elixir, the Magic Pot will become vulnerable and give the player 4000 EXP per hit—more than ten times the normal per-attack rate. The Magic Pot is also one of the best sources of AP in the game, dishing out 1000 AP, which is about four to five times the normal rate (Table 5.1).

Table 5.1 Chocobo Racing Yields[75]

Item	GP
Antarctic Wind	20
Bolt Plume	20
Cat's Bell	500
Chocobracelet	400
Elixir	200
Enemy Away Materia	300
Ether	30
Fire Fang	20
Fire Veil	50
Hero Drink	15
Hi-potion	15
Hyper	10
Ice Crystal	50
Magic Counter Materia	500
Megalixir	300
Phoenix Down	10
Precious Watch	300
Sneak Attack Materia	300
Sprint Shoes	500
Swift Bolt	500
Tranquilizer	50
Turbo Ether	150

Chocobo racing is a great way to earn extra elixirs since they cannot be bought anywhere. In fact, at the S-Rank level (the highest rank of race) the player is twice as likely to get an Elixir as any other reward. It does seem that the designers made this part of the game with this exact conversion in mind.

One of the great things about the chocobo racing mechanics is that there's never any wasted effort because the player never has to accept an item they don't want. All of those undesirable items can actually be converted into the useful currency, GP, which can be spent at most places in the Gold Saucer, including a unique shop in the Wonder Square.

The amount of GP scales depending on the quality of the item, but the purpose of this mechanic is to make every victory useful. GP buys one of the best items in the game, the EXP Plus Materia, which will reduce the amount of grinding the player has to do by directly augmenting earned EXP. There are other ways of acquiring GP to buy this item, like the minigames of the Wonder Square. Like chocobo racing, these games require gil, but they take a lot longer to produce GP than chocobo racing. In the end, all of these paths are ways of converting gil into EXP, either through Magic Pots, augmented EXP income, or both.

For exceptionally skilled and/or knowledgeable players, there are other methods for stockpiling Elixirs than chocobo racing. Players who know where to look can use the Morph command to turn several enemies into Elixirs (although this is grinding, which is what they're probably trying to escape). Players who are preternaturally good at the basketball shooting minigame in the Gold Saucer can rack up GP fairly quickly, too, to buy the EXP Plus Materia. Neither of those things can net the player the unique materia that is strewn about the world map in hidden caves; that is only available through chocobos who can cross terrain that is inaccessible by airship. Those materia are some of the best available in the game, including Mime and Knights of the Round. This is the trick of the chocobo breeding sidequest: it's always giving the player more than one kind of reward. Racing gives the player three rewards: items, GP, and access to higher-level chocobos. Those rewards can be either directly converted into EXP and AP, or else they augment the rates at which EXP and gil come in, giving the player virtually everything they need to face the game's highest challenges.

The last thing to understand about chocobo breeding is that the way it converts one currency to another is cyclical, and that the cycle accelerates. The starting point of the cycle is a surplus of gil which can be spent in the initial costs (housing) or ongoing costs (feeding) of chocobos.

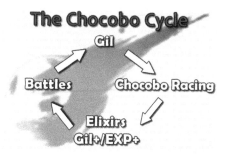

The Chocobo Cycle

Gil

Battles   Chocobo Racing

Elixirs
Gil+/EXP+

Ideally, this cycle will result in the player gaining character levels (and gil) progressively faster and faster. Not only does the EXP Plus Materia directly enhance the rate of acquired experience, but the supply of elixirs and the gil Plus Materia will further enhance the income of EXP and gil, which keeps the cycle going. Players that understand how to use the cycle can gain character levels from 70 to 99 faster than they gained levels from 40 to 70. This is exciting for its own sake; *FFVII* has established a set rate at which players tend to gain levels (of all kinds), and now the player is taking advantage of the game's systems to gain power faster than before. It's also exciting because the optional bosses give shape to the end-game. All that leveling has a point; there's a goal for the player to strive towards. Players who use the chocobo cycle to gain levels faster will be excited to see that their goal (of being powerful enough to defeat Ruby and Emerald Weapon) comes more quickly when they cleverly take advantage of the game's systems.

Other Leveling Tools

Through the chocobo cycle gives the player extra AP through the elixir/Magic Pot conversion, the player is not able to directly augment AP income through that cycle's products. There are other means for accomplishing this, however. Numerous weapons in the game have double AP growth for the materia that are equipped to them, and two weapons have triple growth. The triple-growth weapons are of particular interest here because they're both found rather than bought. Cid's Scimitar is in a fairly obvious treasure box in the submarine base, but Cloud's Apocalypse weapon is located in the optional dungeon, the Ancient Forest. Thus, both of these items are already part of a wide level-up system, in that they are products of diligent exploration. There's also some extra complexity built into their use. The power of these two weapons isn't nearly as high as the game's best equips, so the rate of finishing battles by normal attacks will drop slightly. It's not a huge drop-off, but it does require the player to concentrate on using abilities other than basic attacks. The other drawback to using the triple-growth weapons is that both of them have a small number of materia slots; the Apocalypse has three and the Scimitar has two. This smaller number of slots can deter players who aren't thinking critically about their end-game goals. As we saw above, however, critical thinking is what the designers are trying to reward. The point of the triple-growth weapons is to power up those late-arriving materia like Contain, Mime, EXP Plus, and Knights of the Round. In that function, the triple-growth slots serve quite well, but the player has to consciously make a decision to level a few specific materia. Although JRPGs don't always have a reputation for meaningful decisions, and mid-90s Square RPGs in particular are seen as being too simple, this is an example of an implicit tactical choice. The choice has moved from the battle to the preparation for the battle, but it's still there and it definitely matters.

The last part of the level-up system in phase four I want to address is the usefulness of the two optional dungeons, the Gelnika and the Ancient Forest. In all of the graphs about the difficulty of dungeons, I deliberately left these two out. The reason for this omission is that the structure of the optional dungeons is so different from the structure of the story dungeons. All of the game's mandatory dungeons have to be played from start to finish, and first-time players don't know how long each one will take. Thus, players have to be cautious and conserve resources like items and MP. The two optional dungeons don't operate under the same dynamic. The Gelnika is a dead end, and it's only comprised of four rooms.

The player is never more than two rooms away from the save point at which they can cheaply restore the entire party's HP and MP and save. There's no reason to conserve resources here; tents restore MP too cheaply to necessitate conservative behavior. The Ancient Forest is a little different; it does have an endpoint, but it's also quite short.

After getting the few items this short dungeon has to offer, the Ancient Forest's primary use is for grinding. This can be done in the first screen, so as to maintain access to the world map and the use of tents for cheap restoration.

Because of the structure of the dungeons and the configuration of the enemies in them, both the Ancient Forest and the Gelnika enemies offer decent experience with only moderate risk and time expenditure. The best experience in the game is located in the Northern Crater, specifically in the "swamps" section.

That's fairly deep into the crater, however, and it makes for an inconvenient trip. Moreover, the enemies in the Northern Crater are the most dangerous in the game. Of the two optional dungeons, the Gelnika is the more dangerous, but no battle in that dungeon is likely to wipe the party out instantly. No enemy in the dungeon can cast Ultima, Death, or Level 3 Flare, but there are some fairly powerful attacks. The three variants of the "Unknown" enemy all have attacks with component stats of three which they tend to use as their most common attack. The Unknown 2 routinely inflicts paralysis and confuse. The Unknown 3's most common attacks (with component stats of three) inflicts poison and fury. The Serpent enemy casts Aqualung, which hits the whole party with a component stat of 3.25. Because of these attacks, the Gelnika battles are not easy, but the player doesn't have to worry about conserving MP to heal over the long term because of the easily accessible save point. If the player isn't ready for the Gelnika when they reach phase four, the Ancient Forest works as an easier version of the Gelnika. Enemies in the Ancient Forest are weaker than those in the Gelnika (both in terms of HP and attacks), but provide only about 60% of the EXP and AP that enemies in the Gelnika do. There are two enemies in the Ancient Forest that can use attacks with component stats of 1.25 or higher that cause darkness or poison. This lower level of difficulty and lower level of experience points is better-suited to characters below level 50 that need to grind out some EXP quickly. That said, with the right abilities, players can clear battles in the Ancient Forest in one turn because the enemy HP is lower. While the amount of EXP and gil per battle is lower than in the Gelnika, the amount of EXP and gil per turn or per minute can be higher with the right character set-up.

Why is *FFVII* so Back-Heavy?

The chocobo breeding/racing quest brings back the complexity lost in battle tactics and party composition by giving the player a complicated feedback loop to manipulate in the last phase of the game. Although most of the game is straightforward and requires only a low level of critical thinking, the optional content gives players a lot more to think about if they want to beat the optional bosses without having to invest 20 to 40 extra hours grinding. Accelerating the level-up system is interesting on its own, but the *FFVII* team also decided to do it through something other than battles. It would have been easy for them to simply have sent the player hopping between dungeons where different currencies like EXP, AP, and gil were plentiful in different proportions, but they didn't. Instead, they substituted the process of breeding and racing chocobos for those tasks. Eventually, races can start to feel as repetitive as battles, but by the time the player is getting bored, he or she should be well on the way to the goal of a black or gold chocobo, and should have racked up plenty of items and GP along the way.

This still leaves the following question: Why does the chocobo quest have to come at the end of *FFVII*? The deeper question is: Why does all the complexity of *FFVII* have to come at the end? The answer is the same as it has been in every other aspect of the game. The *FFVII* team's first priorities are telling a meaningful story, crafting compelling characters, and building a persuasive world. Battles, levels, items, and the tactical complexity those things can create are secondary to storytelling. Once the story is almost over and the only thing left to do is defeat Sephiroth, the designers can move complex systems to the fore without impacting their primary goal. Obviously, this is not the only way to construct games; plenty of RPGs have extremely demanding combat and other challenges right in the middle of their plot. The Dark Souls series has a reputation for robust lore and extremely demanding battles, to give one example. Yet, I think it's telling that when people talk about *FFVII*, they talk about their favorite characters or their favorite scenes, whereas when players talk about *Dark Souls*, they talk about their favorite character builds, bosses, and dungeons. Intentional design choices cause this difference.

Understanding Items as Levels

In the previous section, I described every permanent increase in power, including the acquisition of equipment and materia, as a form of level-up. These level-ups are not as frequent or as uniform as character levels, but that's what makes them interesting. This section attempts to compare all of the meaningful levelups in the battle system to character levels, even if that comparison is somewhat imperfect. The general results of this exercise show that comparing weapons to character levels is somewhat meaningful, especially in terms of ultimate weapons. Comparing armor to character levels, however, is not especially meaningful. Comparing materia to character levels reveals a great deal about the nature of spells in *FFVII*. The materia comparison is the most flawed in the sense that when characters gain power through materia, they often (but not always!) have MP costs that complicate the analysis. Nevertheless, there are several ways in which the comparison between character levels and materia shows us something about the game design that would otherwise be obscure. The stat that I like to use to compare one form of level-up to another is called level equivalence (LEQ). The purpose of the stat is to determine how many character levels an item is worth. The comparison works best on weapons. To calculate the LEQ of a weapon, simply find the point in the game at which a character switches from one weapon to another and determine the raw base damage (component stat of one, no defense calculation) of each of those weapons. Then, calculate how many levels the character would have to gain in order to equal the base damage of the new weapon while still equipping the old weapon. Below, I have visualized the LEQ for all of Red XIII's weapons.[76-78]

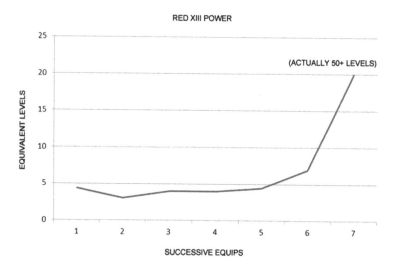

For most of the game, each weapon is worth about four levels, although the number increases slightly as the game goes on up to just about six levels. It's not a huge increase, but it does warrant the spending of gil. The only outlier is the ultimate weapon, which is worth more than 50 levels, meaning that Red XIII would have to be higher than level 99 (which is impossible) to achieve that damage without the weapon. The point is clear, however: ultimate weapons in *FFVII* are ludicrously powerful. Although I didn't visualize them, the same thing is true for the weapons of Cloud, Cid, and Cait Sith. Each weapon increase is only worth a few levels, except for the ultimate weapon, which is more powerful and valuable than any other item in the game.

It's not practically possible to perform LEQ calculations for armor because there is no equivalent of the raw or average damage that are used to calculate the LEQ of weapons. Enemies vary too much in the kind of damage they put out, and in what increments. Materia, on the other hand, are actually easier to perform LEQ calculations for than weapons. The very simple method for this is to look at the component stats of various materia-based abilities and compare them to a hypothetical spell which does base (1x modifier) magic damage. The only complication is that the point at which a player gains access to new weapons is fixed—treasures and vendors come along during certain quests, and there's a fairly clear suggested level for each quest (based on the levels of the enemies in the relevant dungeon). There is no clear indicator in the game that says at what point a player will learn Ice 2, Ice 3, or Flare, however. Therefore for my LEQ calculation, I'm going to use a level 30 Red XIII as the casting character. It's an arbitrary choice, but it is one that is consistently applied.

Spell LEQ

Although it does not take efficiency into account, we can calculate the LEQ of each level of elemental spell in *FFVII*, and thereby understand how many character levels a materia level is worth. To do as much raw damage with Fire 1 as he does with Fire 2, Red XIII would need to gain 99 levels (i.e., the LEQ is, coincidentally, 99). This is impossible, since the cap is 99 and he's already level 30, but extrapolating the statistical trends for the character shows that it would take a level 129 Red XIII to make up the difference in power between Fire and Fire 2. The LEQ of Fire 3 versus Fire 2 is 80, meaning that Red XIII would have to be level 110 to make up the difference in raw damage between the two spells. In other words, the loss of MP efficiency is completely justified given the amount of power of each level of spell. So each level gained by a basic elemental materia is worth upwards of 70 character levels in damage (if you don't take MP into account).

The tactical significance of spell choice gets deeper when spells target more than one enemy at a time. For normal magic (green materia) spells augmented by the All Materia, the damage formula is simple: raw spell damage is cut in half. Certain materia do not incur this penalty, however. Most of the unaffected spells are summons, but a few are enemy skills. For example, what is the difference between casting Fire 2/All, Ifrit, and Beta? All of these are multi-target fire spells, but there are differences in both LEQ and MP spent (Table 5.2).

Table 5.2 LEQ of Various Spells[79]

Spell 1	Damage	Spell 2	Damage	Difference	How Many Levels Would You Have to Gain for Equivalence?
Fire 2 (all)	339	Ifrit	764	429	57 levels
Fire 2 (all)	339	Beta	1528	1189	214 level
Fire 3 (all)	508	Beta	1528	1020	28 levels

When cast by a level 30 Red XIII, Fire 2/All's raw damage is about 339 to each enemy. At the same level, Ifrit does about 764 raw damage to all targets (because it isn't affected by split damage mechanics), for an LEQ of 57. Beta, the enemy skill used by the Midgar Zolom, is also not affected by the split damage mechanic to which Fire/Fire 2 is subjected. It does about 1,528 raw magic damage, for a surprisingly large LEQ of 214 versus the Fire 2 spell. The Fire 2 spell is the cheapest in terms of MP, but it's only 13 MP cheaper than Beta, despite its much lower power when cast on multiple targets. Against a multi-target Fire 3, Beta still has an LEQ of 28 (i.e., in order to beat the damage of Beta at level 30, Red XIII would need to be level 58 when casting Fire 3/All), despite costing 20 fewer MP, making it a vastly superior choice for clearing multiple targets.

Why design Beta and Ifrit to be better than the Fire spells of similar level? The goal is discovery (i.e., wide levels) rather than choice. A great deal of RPG design comes down to making the right choice at the right time; this is a trait that RPGs inherited from their wargame ancestors. Unfortunately, the choice between spells like Fire 3 and Beta isn't a very meaningful one. Fire 3 is a little better than Beta against single targets, and Beta is more efficient than Fire 3 against multiple targets. It's important for players to notice this and choose accordingly, but it's not a particularly deep and meaningful decision. Instead of awarding power to players who make the best decisions, the designers are awarding power to the players who explore the game the most thoroughly. The Fire Materia is acquired through any of several materia shops. The Ifrit summon is obtained through beating a mandatory boss, but it is unique. The Beta ability can only be obtained by surviving the attack when it is cast by one of the few creatures that uses it in random battles. Each one of these abilities is harder to obtain than the last, and so it makes sense that they would have varying levels of power. That's the whole point of a wide level-up system.

Independent Materia and LEQ

Independent materia, which include such gems as Magic Plus or HP Plus, are the easiest kind of equip to measure by LEQ. The low effort required to measure them reflects the low effort that went into balancing them. The strange inequality of these materia shows up pretty clearly in any comparative graph. Below is a graph of the LEQ of three different kinds of independent materia affecting three different character stats on a level 30 Red XIII.[80,81]

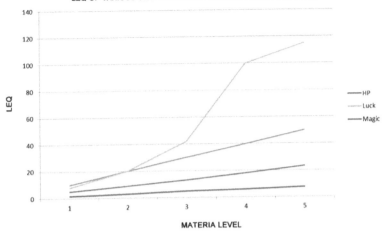

In the graph, each of these materia is at master level, granting a 50% bonus to a particular stat. Because the growth rate for each of these stats is so different, a 50% boost can have wildly different results in terms of equivalent levels gained. For example, a level 30 Red XIII will have an average luck stat of about 18 (stats can vary a little bit in different playthroughs). A level 99 Red XIII has a luck stat of about 24. Therefore, a 50% boost to luck at level 30 is worth more than 60 levels. On the other hand, HP grows a lot per level, so a 50% increase is only equivalent to gaining approximately eight levels worth of HP. A growth of 50% means something very different for each stat. The designers did seem to spot the discrepancy between luck and HP to some degree; the Luck Plus Materia requires twice as much AP to master as the HP Plus Materia.

Where the designers failed to notice a difference is in the Magic Plus Materia. Mastering the Magic Plus Materia requires the same amount of AP as the HP Plus Materia, but it allows Red XIII to cast magic as though he were 23 levels higher. If the Magic Plus Materia were hard to find, this would be another example of the enhanced power of wide levels, but this is not the case.

Although slightly out of the way, the Magic Plus Materia is visible from the main path through an obligatory dungeon. It's certainly within the realm of possibility that the designers didn't care that this materia was more powerful than others in its group. It's equally possible that they applied a template to it without checking the math. In this case, LEQ shows where there is still a nail sticking up out of the floorboards, so to speak.

Using LEQ in Other Games

The point of the *Reverse Design* series is to make available to its readers the design tools that were used in the making of classic games. On its face, this is an impossible task, because the "tools" that the *FFVII* team used were probably the subjective judgments of people like Hironobu Sakaguchi, Yoshinori Kitase, Hiromichi Tanaka, and Yasushi Matsumura. In lieu of having those people on the staff making your game, I have tried to create tools that faithfully recapture their creative output, even if these tools cannot replicate their creative judgment. The LEQ stat is one such tool, although it has its limitations. The LEQ value works best for one-to-one comparisons, like one weapon or spell against another of its kind, but it's still useful for broader analysis of a game. Using LEQ shows us that exploration was mathematically more important to the designers of FFVII than grinding. The ultimate weapons, none of which require grinding to obtain, are usually worth more than 50 levels. The most useful enemy skills, which are worth 20 to 100+ levels, require no grinding to obtain; they require exploration. The most useful independent materia are easy to find and a little overpowered. There is no "correct" LEQ for any given weapon or spell, but LEQ can tell you when items are statistical outliers that might destroy the game balance you've worked so hard on. This tool doesn't turn us into Sakaguchi and Kitase, but it does help us to measure our work against theirs in a meaningful and precise way.

6

Enemy Archetypes

Having seen all the phases and what they offer, I want to try reverse-engineering some design templates for non-boss enemies in *FFVII*. The graphs in the previous sections only provide averages for each stat in a quest. Averages are useful for understanding what a whole quest is like in aggregate, but they don't always explain how individual enemies contribute toward the overall feel of each battle, quest or the game at large. At the same time, it wouldn't be useful to describe every individual enemy as a piece of unique content because there's too much noise in that. Instead, I've derived six archetypes of enemies found in *FFVII*. These archetypes cover about two-thirds of all the non-boss battles in the game. There are some enemies which don't fit into any category. Some of these enemies are gimmicky, like the Ying & Yang, Mover, or Magic Pot enemies, who all have highly unusual abilities or defenses. Some of these enemies are extreme versions of game design concepts, like the Bomb and Grenade, who keep getting more dangerous throughout the fight. Some enemies are in place only to be hunted, like the Beach Plug. The majority of *FFVII* enemies fall into some kind of archetype.

The One-Two Punch

The most basic enemy archetype is what I call the "one-two punch" (OTP) type, and so I will use this type to explain how the template works. The first thing to notice is the behavior summary. The basic design idea behind the OTP is that it has a normal attack that does base damage, but it also uses a second ability—a special attack that does 1.25 to three times base damage. I call this ability the "signature" attack or ability, as it is the thing that defines most of the archetypes. The OTP tends to use its basic attack and signature attack interchangeably.[16, 82–84]

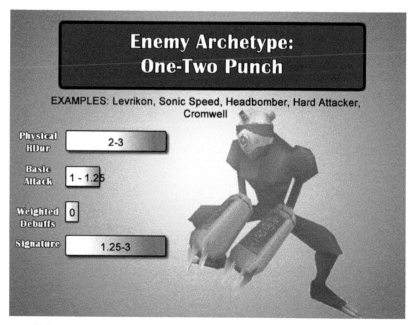

(N.B. every archetype in this section is derived from these same sources)

The rest of the card is fairly simple. The top row shows the number of basic attacks required to defeat this enemy by Red XIII at the same level with the appropriate gear. Like everything else on the card, this row has a range of values because not every enemy of an archetype is exactly the same. Note that although the range is displayed in highest-to-lowest order, that's not necessarily chronological. As we saw in the discussions of phases two and three, different monster attributes peak at different times. The range simply covers the quests up until the final dungeon and optional content. The next row shows the component stat for the enemy's basic attack, which is the most common attack all enemies use. Sometimes the basic attack is magical, but most of the time it's physical. Sometimes, an enemy's basic attack is below base damage—it has a component stat of less than one—but usually it's one or higher. The next row on the card shows the range of component stats for the OTP's special ability, which is between one and three. Note that although the high end for a special ability of the OTP is a component stat of three, this actually happens in phase three, not in phase four. On the other hand, the enemy with the highest component stat for this category (the Sculpture from the Whirlwind Maze) also has a low end durability score of two. The enemy with the highest durability from this group is from the Northern Crater.

The Rabid Fox

Another simple type of enemy is the rabid fox family of enemies, which inflict the majority of the game's debuffs. The typical setup for the rabid fox is that it has a basic attack which it mixes interchangeably with a signature attack that also inflicts a debuff.

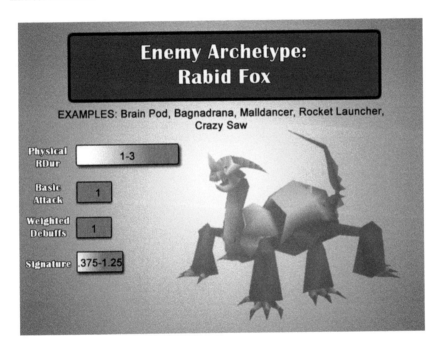

Note that the signature ability still does damage. In phases one and two, the component stats for the debuff-inflicting abilities are below one, but by the end of the game these abilities grow to the point where they are even with (or sometimes slightly above) base damage. Interestingly, the basic attack for these creatures does not grow, but instead stays locked at base damage levels. Typically, the rabid fox type of enemy inflicts debuffs to which I gave a ranking of "1"—debuffs like poison, slow, frog, and blind. Finally, although it isn't listed on the card, I want to point out a trend in the AI of these enemies. Most enemies of this type use their debuff ability as part of a random mix of abilities that includes their basic attack.

Sometimes, however, enemies of this type will continuously use their debuff ability until all party members are afflicted, even if this is an impossible goal because some party members are immune.

The Scatter-Shot

The scatter-shot type is built around a medium-low-strength attack that hits all party members. The component stat for this signature attack is almost always around 1.25. The most common durability score for these enemies is three normal attacks by an appropriately leveled and equipped Red XIII. The durability of this type of enemy varies a lot across the game, sometimes high and sometimes low, irrespective of how late in the game this enemy appears.

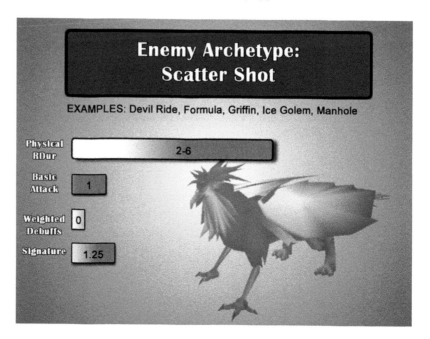

Enemy Archetype: Scatter Shot

EXAMPLES: Devil Ride, Formula, Griffin, Ice Golem, Manhole

Physical RDur	2-6
Basic Attack	1
Weighted Debuffs	0
Signature	1.25

The up-and-down fluctuation in difficulty that is the bedrock of videogame design appears frequently in *FFVII*, and the design of this enemy across the game is another example of that. Finally, the basic attacks for this type of enemy usually only do base damage.

The Magic Imp

The magic imp has three primary characteristics: relatively low durability, the ability to do high damage, and a large suite of abilities to choose from. The durability score for these enemies can range from one to five hits from an appropriately leveled Red XIII at various points across the course of the game.

That fact can be a little misleading, however, because the only enemy in this class with a durability score above four is the Harpy enemy, which always appears as the only enemy in a battle. Its higher durability is probably a function of its solitude. For the most part, the durability of these enemies is three or below. Additionally, these enemies tend to have attacks with component stats between two and five, meaning that they can deal large amounts of damage, although they only tend to do target one party member at a time. The last important characteristic of the magic imp is that they have a large suite of abilities to pick from, typically including at least one ability that inflicts a debuff.

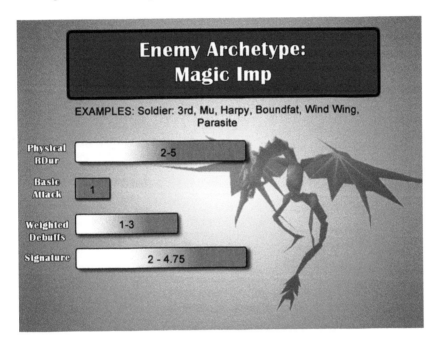

Enemy Archetype:
Magic Imp

EXAMPLES: Soldier: 3rd, Mu, Harpy, Boundfat, Wind Wing, Parasite

Physical RDur	2-5
Basic Attack	1
Weighted Debuffs	1-3
Signature	2 - 4.75

Normally this means having several abilities with different component stats, different elemental affinities or both. With such a large set of abilities to pick from, combined with relatively low durability, a magic imp-type enemy will not always cast its debuff or strongest ability before dying.

The Titan

The titan type is an enemy that appears alone in battle, has a high durability score, usually has a powerful multi-target attack, and often uses low-level debuffs. Essentially, the titan enemy is an entire battle contained in one creature. The titan's defining characteristic is its high durability score, always above nine physical attacks, but going as high as 14. Although there are plenty of non-titan battles in the game that have that same total durability spread across several enemies, the titan is more dangerous. Several enemies with medium durability can attack more often than one enemy with high durability, but one good multi-target spell can wipe many or all of them out, making the battle shorter and easier. There's no shortcut around a titan; most of the time, the player will not have access to any spell powerful enough to instantly kill a titan at the same level as their party members. Because the titan is going to survive a few rounds, it will almost certainly use all of its abilities at least once. The first titan in the game has a weak basic attack, but after that the component stat for the titans' basic attack is about two. The signature attack is where the titans really deal their damage, however. Most of the titans use a multi-target spell that has a component stat somewhere between 3.75 and six. Their behavior scripts are set up so that they cast this spell at least once, though they often cast it several times in a battle. Additionally, many of these signature attacks inflict a debuff, most commonly darkness.

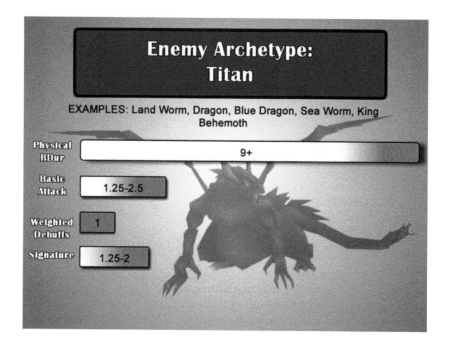

If the signature spell does not inflict a debuff, the titan will usually have some other ability which does, although the debuff is always of a lesser one-turn type.

One odd point about the titan type is that although it offers an above-average amount of EXP per battle, it actually offers a below-average amount of EXP per attack (i.e., per durability). I find this to be odd because it means the hardest challenges give the least reward on a rate basis. This datum does at least give us the insight that maybe the designers of that time weren't calculating by rate guidelines, even if the game balance came out as though they were doing so.

Killer Rabbit

The killer rabbit type is a weak enemy that comes in large numbers. Although the durability score for these enemies is always low, their primary characteristic is the low component stats of their attacks. Sometimes, the signature attack of a killer rabbit will apply a debuff, but more often it does not. On paper, this type of enemy can look a little bit like the rabid fox, but the lower durability and inconsistent debuff usage differentiate it. In actual usage, the killer rabbit becomes very distinct, as it usually comes in groups of four or more. This enemy type also demonstrates an unusual trend in EXP disbursement. The killer rabbit is a great source of phase-two EXP, not because it offers such a great per-turn rate of EXP, but because it comes in large groups and has a low durability. One low-cost multi-target spell can wipe a group of these enemies out in one turn. Thus, by driving down the amount of time per battle, the player can drive up EXP income per minute. Killer rabbits disappear after phase two, however.

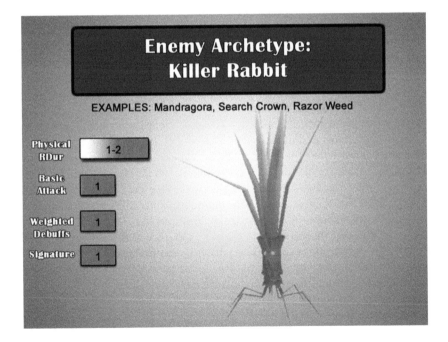

Enemy Archetype: Killer Rabbit

EXAMPLES: Mandragora, Search Crown, Razor Weed

Physical RDur	1-2
Basic Attack	1
Weighted Debuffs	1
Signature	1

As players gain an increasing number of powerful multi-target attacks toward the end of phase two, it would be too easy for them to plow through battles like these and collect a lot of EXP. Plus, the puny damage this enemy puts out wouldn't fit with the design philosophy of phase three at all.

Enemies to Order

Enemies that fit into one of the archetypes listed above account for 70% of the total enemies encountered in phases two, three, and four of *FFVII*. (Phase one, being a tutorial, isn't like the other phases in a number of ways and would unhelpfully skew any analysis of them.) That leaves a sizeable chunk of enemies that don't fall into an archetype. These remaining enemies do exhibit some patterns, but these patterns don't necessarily constitute a new archetype. I call these "enemies to order," as they tend to fill in a wide variety of needs for the designer. The most common type of enemy to order is simply an archetypal enemy with an extra ability appended to it. The Nibel Wolf, for example, is an OTP-type with a revive ability added on. The Hell Rider VR2 is an OTP-type with the ability to move party members from front to back row and vice-versa. Another kind of enemy to order is one that simply combines the abilities of two other archetypes. The Custom Sweeper and Death Machine (which, interestingly, have the same enemy model) are both a combination of the OTP and scatter-shot types. A few enemies to order are reduced versions of archetypes. For example, a couple of enemies operate like the titan type in the way they attack but lack the requisite high durability. A few enemies are like the OTP or rabid fox types except with the basic attack removed, leaving only the signature attack. The important thing to notice is that the archetypes are still the basis for most of the enemies in the game, even when those enemies technically fall outside the strictest definition of a type.

The only group of enemies that doesn't somehow relate to an archetype is the one that relies on defensive tactics. This group does not belong to an archetype because they are few in number and inconsistent in execution. Some of these enemies cast barriers on themselves like the Adamantaimai; some have gimmicky defenses that greatly reduce damage, like the Yin/Yang. Some of these enemies have normal defenses and only ever counterattack. The thing that prevents them from being a defined group is that they lack attacks in common. Neither their stats, component stats, nor attack types have any common theme, and therefore the player's experience of these enemies isn't the same as the player's experience of the Titan. Moreover, although this entire group of enemies uses defense-oriented tactics, their durability scores can be either quite high or quite low. In other words, they rely on one-off gimmicks, and gleaning lessons from those is problematic in any game.

The Distribution of Enemy Types

Although the explanation of *FFVII*'s phases gives the best explanation for the player's experience of the game, there are a few trends in the distribution of enemy archetypes that give a little more insight into how those phases were crafted. The first thing to examine is the precise distribution of each enemy type across the whole game. Except for one factor, it is unsurprising.

6. Enemy Archetypes

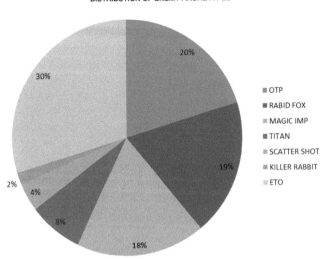

The OTP, rabid fox, and magic imp make up the majority of the game's enemies. The titan is a little rarer, as it should be, considering its power and the fact that it is a whole battle by itself. The enemy to order (ETO) slice of the graph is large, which makes sense since that portion includes lots of different kinds of enemies, but it's not so large as to make archetypes irrelevant. The killer rabbit archetype is a very small proportion of the total enemy population because it only exists in phase two. In that phase, the killer rabbit performs an important and clear function, however, so it's worth mentioning. For different reasons, the scatter-shot type is a remarkably small proportion of the whole enemy population. Although pure scatter-shot types are few, the scatter-shot type serves as the basis for a large number of enemies-to-order. Usually, this means that a scatter-shot type gets one extra ability, like a counterattack, a final attack, a debuff, or some kind of heal or shield spell. In spite of all those extra abilities it might have, the scatter shot's signature (and most common) move is still to hit the entire party for medium damage.

There are several trends that reveal a few significant things about enemy archetypes. The most obvious trend is that the incidence of the rabid fox enemy type declines across the course of the game.

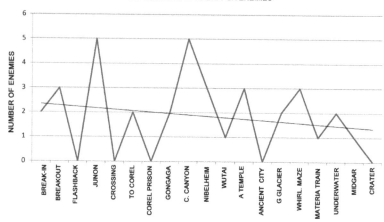

This makes sense since phase two is the part of the game during which debuffs peak. The rabid fox type enemies, who inflict the majority of the game's debuffs, are used less when debuffs (especially low-level debuffs) aren't as prevalent. The rabid fox type does make a slight comeback at the end of the game when debuff prevalence rises again, but at that point, the magic imp and titan are applying many of the debuffs as well. Although the magic imp often has a debuff as well, it's less likely to use it in any given battle. Nevertheless, many of the debuffs in phase four are inflicted by magic imps or titans.

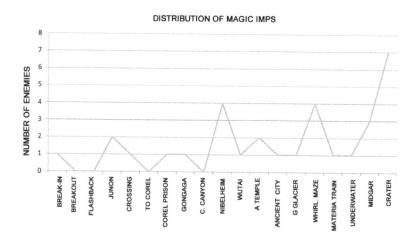

Titans tend to use lower-level debuffs like darkness, but there are quite a few of them in the late game, so players who are not immune to such debuffs will suffer from them.

There are also a couple of trends that seem like they might logically happen but which do not actually occur. Being the most difficult type of battle, one might expect the prevalence of titans to steadily rise across the course of the game. This supposition, although intuitive, is not borne out by the data except in one quest.

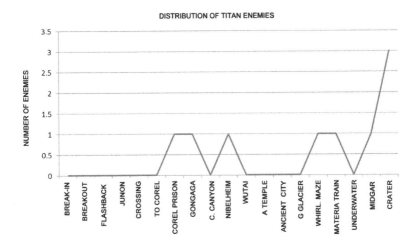

The number of titans per quest stays the same until the final dungeon, at which point it does go up markedly, but for most of the game, there is just one titan per quest (if there are any at all). This follows with the trend of average battle length per quest, which never really goes higher than nine basic attacks at any time during the game. One might expect the game to get linearly more difficult, but *FFVII* relies more on qualitative changes than quantitative brute force. Similarly, the prevalence of enemies-to-order does not climb too much across the course of the game.

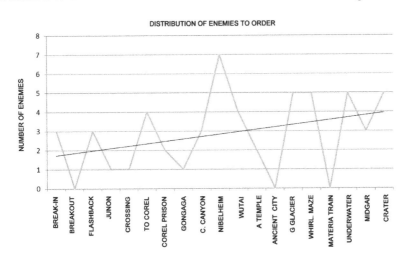

The ETO type peaks in prevalence at Nibelheim and then declines a bit before leveling off for the rest of the game. One might logically expect that ETOs, who are often combinations or enhanced versions of other types, would become increasingly prevalent across the course of the game. Up to a point, that's true, but even in the last dungeons, the designers don't abandon the use of enemy archetypes. There's a great lesson in that, I think. The hardest challenges in a game should come at the end of that game, but that doesn't mean that the designers should introduce challenges that break the patterns established elsewhere in the game. Players will put up with almost any increase in difficulty as long as it is gradual and as long as those challenges—though greater—are familiar to what they have already seen.

7

The Design of Towns and Dungeons

One of the great pleasures of the digital RPG is the ability to explore the invented world of the game. Even in games that are otherwise flawed, exploring a large and well-realized world can make the experience worthwhile. Plenty of critics have remarked how generic the plot of *FFVII* is, and I agree that a general outline of the plot is fairly formulaic. Superhuman villains are always trying to ascend to godhood in RPGs (whether Western or Japanese), and a ragtag bunch of heroes is always rising up to stop them. Like many great RPGs, *FFVII* distinguishes itself through interesting characters, meaningful themes, and memorable places. This chapter of the book focuses on the last of those three elements. Although graphics technology has progressed a great deal since *FFVII* came out, the artistic and ludic techniques that the *FFVII* team used in creating their virtual world are still relevant. Because indie JRPGs are growing in popularity, these techniques have become extremely relevant to a sector of the game development industry that does not adhere to the highest graphical standard. If there is one lesson to take away from this chapter, it is that the *FFVII* team put the artistic sense of place ahead of orthodox RPG dungeon and town design ideas much of the time. We'll see how that dynamic influences the design of maps throughout the game.

Although *FFVII* does lots of idiosyncratic things with its towns and dungeons, it does not entirely abandon the standard framework of RPG town and dungeon design. Towns are full of NPCs, but in accordance with JRPG norms, those NPCs do not dispense quests like they might in an open-world Western RPG. Dungeons are full of loot, although as is the case in most JRPGs, that loot is scattered about the dungeon rather than being hoarded behind the dungeon boss. That scattering has an important effect: the dungeons are consequently wide, and players have to do more exploring if they want to get all the best loot. *Final Fantasy VII* is not the first game in the series to design dungeons this way—not by a long shot. Nevertheless, *FFVII* takes the generic conventions of dungeon design and goes to great lengths to incorporate them into artistically persuasive settings.

Defining Maps and Map Elements

First, some definitions. Three elements shape a dungeon or town: the size and number of its maps, the item contents, and the encounter rate (for dungeons) or NPC population (for towns). The trickiest task is defining the size of each map in a town or dungeon since these maps are unequal in several ways. I divide all maps into four sizes: small, medium, large, and huge. The definitions aren't precise to the level of a single footstep, but there are some useful guidelines that I employ. Small maps tend to be single confined rooms with large amounts of unlit margin around them.

Medium rooms are between one and two standard-resolution screens large when Cloud's avatar is normal sized. These rooms are not always neatly shaped, however. Often, two small rooms adjoin each other on the same screen, and I count that as a medium map because the overall size roughly fills one to two screens.

Large maps tend to be bigger than two screens if Cloud were a normal size. There are two kinds of large maps, for the most part. One kind of large map shows Cloud change size as he gets further away from the camera, to imply the amount of distance he covers. On the other kind of large map, the camera will track Cloud as he moves across it, but the amount of tracking is significant and will show several screens worth of background before Cloud reaches the other side. In both cases, however, the map should only take a few seconds to cross if the attempt is not interrupted by an event or battle.

Huge maps are the signature size of *FFVII*, although they're not the most numerous type of map. The huge map is where most of the really interesting trends in *FFVII* map design are found. A huge map has three characteristics. First, a huge map tends to extend all the way to the edge of the screen without much black space in the margin (although there are a few exceptions to this). Second, a huge map is usually so big that the camera has to track Cloud for at least three seconds as he crosses it. Third, the camera is zoomed out so that Cloud's avatar appears tiny on the screen. The best example of these maps is in Midgar, where the hyperbolic architecture is an essential part of the feeling of the game.

Although there aren't many of these maps in the game, their impact and detail are a key part of the persuasiveness of the game-world.

The other important thing to understand before examining individual maps is the encounter rate in dungeons. Strangely, encounter rate is one of the least-documented aspects of *FFVII*. Because the game is old, famous, and systems-oriented, there is a lot of documentation about it online. Even examinations of the decompiled code of *FFVII* (which have been an incredible help to the writing of this book) fail to completely document the way that encounters work. The basic idea is that after Cloud takes a certain number of steps, a pre-defined integer is added to a running total. That running total is compared to a random number between one and 255. When the running total exceeds the random number, a battle begins. After the battle, the running total is cleared and the process starts over. It would look like this Table 7.1:

Table 7.1 Random Encounter Mechanics Test

Movement Counter	Random Rolls	Encounter
32	148	NO
64	95	NO
96	201	NO
128	157	NO
164	101	YES
0	217	NO

What isn't known is how many steps Cloud has to take before incurring another cumulative increment. The player-character appears to be able to take approximately 12 steps before the counter begins incrementing. How the counter increments after that is not clear. It does not appear that every step after the first 12 (again, this is approximate) increments the counter, or else the number of steps would vary much more than it did during several large samples that I took. This does not make the picture much clearer, however. The size of increments which get added to the running total is fixed, but the number of steps required for the counter to move up by an increment is unknown. In fact, it's not clear whether individual steps are counted towards the next increment or whether Cloud's entire

7. The Design of Towns and Dungeons

run-cycle is the basic unit. Without further examination of the decompiled code by those who possess it directly, it may not be possible to know.

The good news is that the relative rate of random encounters is measurable. That is, we can measure one map's rate of encounters against another map's rate of encounters. The way that the designers control the rate of random encounters is by increasing the size of the increment that occurs every time the player's avatar takes the unknown number of steps. If the increment increases from 32 to 48, the average number of steps before the player hits a random encounter will be reduced (i.e., the battles will come more frequently). The key word in the previous sentence is average; because the encounter formula checks against a random variable that is between one and 255, it can make the encounter rate in an area feel higher or lower than it actually is for a couple of reasons. One reason is small sample sizes. Unless the player is grinding, they will not encounter enough battles to really determine what the encounter rate is. There's just too much random noise for a small number of encounters to reveal the underlying trend. The other reason why a player might not properly understand the encounter rate of a given map is that almost every dungeon in the game contains maps of varying encounter rates. Sometimes the difference between two screens in the same dungeon can be quite high. We'll examine why this variation should exist in another sub-section below.

Before we get to the granular data, I want to briefly look at encounter rates for the whole game. Although one of the central theses of this book is that *FFVII* does not get more difficult in a linear fashion across the course of the game, there is one place where that is not entirely true. Over time, the rate of random encounters goes up. Below is a graph of the median encounter rate of each successive dungeon in *FFVII*.

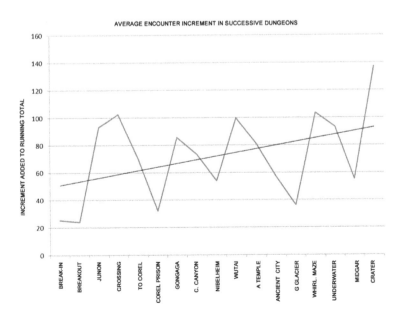

Encounter rates go up over time, although they don't do so uniformly. Again, we see the up and down motion that is the foundation of all videogame design. We also see again that most of the gains in encounter rate occur as the floor for encounter rate rises, rather than the ceiling. After gaining access to the world map for the first time, the only quest with an exceptionally high encounter rate is in the last dungeon.

Size and Setting

The size of maps tells us much about the artistic intent of the *FFVII* design team in several ways. The most important thing to know about map sizes is that except for small rooms, size does not correlate significantly with progress through the game. Instead, maps seem to serve specific narrative requirements that the designers want to convey via setting. To visualize this trend, I have created a graph that shows the composition of each quest's maps by size (in percent).

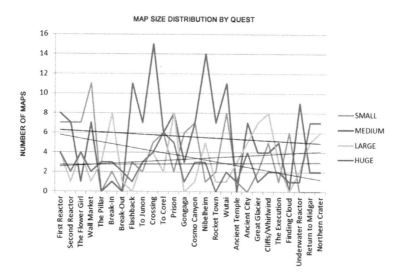

Only one of those trend lines has a significant slope—the "small" map size. Small maps mostly show up in towns, and there is only one new town after Meteor is summoned, so that downward trend makes obvious sense. For the rest of the map sizes, there is very little change in distribution across the course of the game. At a more granular level, though, there is a lot to learn.

When it comes to individual dungeons, the only real trend that sticks out in terms of battles is the lower encounter rate that huge maps have. Relative to the maps in which they appear, huge maps have a slightly lower rate of encounters than small, medium or large maps in the same dungeon. (Indeed, this is what made me sure that huge maps were a meaningfully distinct category.) The dip is not major in most cases, but across the game, huge maps have an encounter rate at least 20% lower than the rest of the dungeon. Because of their lower encounter rate, huge maps will throw roughly the same number of encounters at the player as large maps on a per-map basis. The lower encounter rate on huge maps is another example of the same lesson we keep learning about *FFVII*: storytelling is the most important thing to the design team.

The point of huge maps isn't to make a dungeon significantly longer, or else huge maps would have the same encounter rate as the rest of the dungeon. The point of huge maps is to establish context for the dungeon—to make a fantastic place feel persuasive as a fictional setting. Because they show a zoomed-out view of a very large section of a dungeon, huge maps help the player see the dungeon as more than a mere collection of treasure rooms.

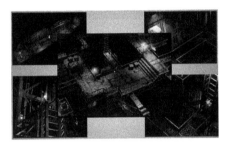 

The one or two huge maps in most dungeons help the player's subconscious to organize a dungeon in a meaningful way. From a practical perspective, this is useful for navigation purposes. It's easier to remember where a huge and artistically distinct map is located than it is to remember where several small, similar rooms are. This mental map also embellishes the sense of setting. These days we are inundated with procedurally-generated RPG dungeons. Those dungeons are great for making each trip through that dungeon feel fresh in a purely practical sense, but their random permutations can often feel inauthentic as a fictional setting. *Final Fantasy VII* shows us the exact opposite of this; dungeons are constructed to feel persuasive, but they are only new once.

Exceptions to Sizing Rules and What They Mean

There are a few adjustments I make for context when measuring maps that affect the granular data that comes in the section below. I already defined what map sizes usually mean, but I want to reveal some of the mitigating factors that affect my calculations. For instance, some maps play a lot smaller than they appear. This isn't common, but it does happen. The best example is in Cosmo Canyon, where there is an overlook which shows the entire surrounding area. This is a large screen, but Cloud can only move around a very small part of it.

Thus, I don't call this a huge map, but rather a small map—a big difference. Although the camera has to track Cloud as he moves, the actual amount of explorable space is limited to a small path that can be traversed in a few seconds. I rate this map as being medium rather than huge; although the map file itself is huge, the player has a very limited space in which to move. A similar case occurs at the Gaea Cliffs, and only happens when the player is on the small ledges that lead in and out of the cave system. Because it's a dungeon screen, I dropped the size rating to take into account the fact that most of the map is encounter-free, and therefore much quicker than a dungeon map of this size would ordinarily be.

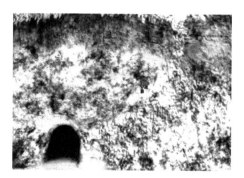

The cliff screens are some of the largest in the game in terms of pure pixel space, but they don't feel that way because the player doesn't face random encounters while climbing. Random encounters only happen when the player is on the small ledges that lead in and out of the cave system. Because it's a dungeon screen, I dropped the size rating to take into account the fact that most of the map is encounter-free, and therefore much quicker than a dungeon map of this size would ordinarily be.

The Distribution of Map Sizes

Size is not everything, but the sizes of maps in *FFVII* give us some useful information about the way that towns and dungeons are constructed. Below is a graph which shows the overall breakdown of map sizes in *FFVII*.

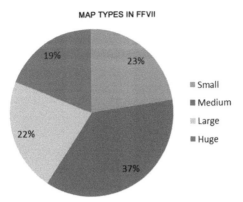

MAP TYPES IN FFVII

- Small
- Medium
- Large
- Huge

The distribution is fairly even for small, large, and huge maps at roughly 20% each. Medium maps are the majority by a significant amount. As far as I can tell, this is just an instance of a standard distribution. Most data points in most graphs tend to cluster near the middle of the data set, but does this hold up at a more granular level?

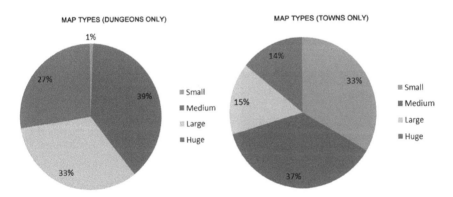

MAP TYPES (DUNGEONS ONLY)

- Small
- Medium
- Large
- Huge

MAP TYPES (TOWNS ONLY)

- Small
- Medium
- Large
- Huge

The separate graphs for towns and dungeons look quite different, except when it comes to medium maps, which are basically unchanged (38% and 37%, respectively). If we simply must have an artistic (rather than statistical) reason why medium maps are so prevalent, I would say that it probably stems from the size of the screen. Most medium maps are between one and two screens large (when Cloud is normal-sized). It makes sense that this natural boundary would influence the design of maps and lead to more medium-sized locations for reasons of convenience for the artists and programmers.

For all other sizes, the two graphs tell a more complex story. Small maps make up a much larger percentage of town maps (33%) than they do dungeon maps (8%). This is a significant historical change. In earlier *Final Fantasies*, there were many small "treasure trove" maps (such as in *FFVI*, below).

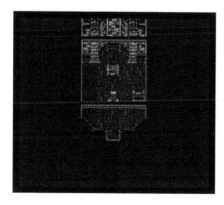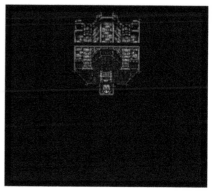

It's tempting to think that this is a structural feature as well. Did the *FFVII* designers remove small rooms in dungeons to reduce the amount of time the player spends waiting for those rooms to load? It sounds plausible, but if that were the case, they probably would have decreased the amount of small rooms in the game generally. Yet, there are more small maps than large or huge ones. I think that instead of a structural concern, this is an artistic decision. It's easy to understand why the game has small maps if we remember that storytelling is the prevailing concern of the designers.

If one of the central goals of *FFVII*'s maps is to reinforce the theme of people who have lost their old lives, then these small maps do a good job of it. This also explains why small maps are so much more prevalent in towns. Confined spaces like these have a greater impact when there's someone in them. The presence of NPCs makes the small map feel even smaller for being crowded. This is the only practical way to create crowded spaces in *FFVII*. The original PlayStation hardware couldn't support a ton of NPCs in one place, so the location itself has to be smaller so that a few NPCs fill it up. It's only natural that there are more small rooms where people live—in towns. That said, there are actually a few NPCs living in dungeon areas, and they usually occupy small maps, too.

7. The Design of Towns and Dungeons

If anything, this confirms the effect. Both of the screenshots above show maps that are much smaller than the average room in the dungeon to which they belong.

Where the Loot Lies

Dungeons are more than empty spaces filled with monsters. From the very beginning of RPG history, designers have scattered loot throughout dungeons to make them worth exploring. There are many ways to examine the distribution of loot throughout dungeons in *FFVII*, but since we just looked at map sizes, I'll start there. The most important datum about the relationship between map size and treasure disposition is that huge and large maps have most of the treasure. Huge maps have slightly more treasure than large ones, but the difference between huge and large is nothing compared to the difference between those two categories and medium maps. Despite being the most common map-size in dungeons (and everywhere else), medium and small maps have a lot less treasure. This explains the philosophy of maps in *FFVII* pretty clearly: the bigger maps are meant to be explored from edge to edge.

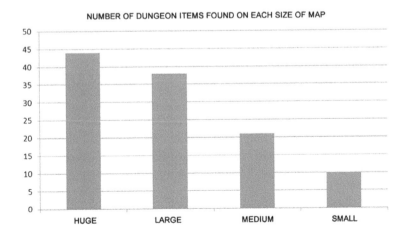

NUMBER OF DUNGEON ITEMS FOUND ON EACH SIZE OF MAP

By sticking treasure all around large and huge maps, the player has a reason to get off the critical path and take the risk of exploring. Based on everything else we have seen in *FFVII*, we can safely assume that one of the motivations for the scattering of loot throughout the dungeon is to make the player see the lovingly-crafted settings that the *FFVII* team spent so much time on.

Exploration also forces more combat, obviously, and I don't want to rule that out, either. In an RPG, a player needs to level their characters up, and in *FFVII* that's mostly done by fighting. (Indeed, in phase four, the player needs to do more leveling and gear hunting than normal. We'll see shortly how huge maps become a little more prevalent to answer this need at the end of the game.) By sticking treasure all around large and huge maps, the player has a reason to get off the critical path and take the risk of exploring. Based on everything else we have seen in *FFVII*, we can safely assume that one of the motivations for the scattering of loot throughout the dungeon is to make the player see the lovingly-crafted settings that the *FFVII* team spent so much time on. Exploration also forces more combat, obviously, and I don't want to rule that out, either. In an RPG, a player needs to level their characters up, and in *FFVII* (as I mentioned earlier) that's mostly done by fighting.

Just placing treasure chests on the map is not enough to incentivize players to seek them out; the contents of the chests have to be worth the journey. On large and huge maps, about 53% of the treasure is either an equippable item or a new materia. The rest of the items are of the consumable type like potions, grenades, etc. Some of those items are useful, but the player will almost certainly be happier to find a weapon that can be used more than once—or even better, materia that can be used for the rest of the game. The composition of loot types in towns is different: only 43% of loot in towns is an equip or materia. The difference isn't staggering, but it does reveal an important design dynamic. Treasure in towns doesn't have to be as valuable because there are no random encounters to make its retrieval a burden. In dungeons, however, the treasure distribution favors (at least slightly) items that are useful for a long time or in order to entice players to spend time searching for it.

While we are on the topic of loot in towns versus loot in dungeons, there are a few interesting trends that appear in a more granular comparison of the two pools of loot. The most important (and least surprising) trend is the increase in dungeon loot relative to town loot as the game goes on. As the player gets deeper into the game, their stamina for dungeons grows, and so more of the loot can appear as a part of areas with monster encounters. The dungeon with the most overall loot is the final dungeon, which is exactly what we would suspect from an *FF* title.

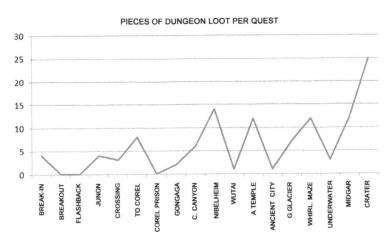

We see the kind of up-and-down variation that has been common to most facets of *FFVII*, even if it doesn't really match up with the four phases of the game very closely. When isolating materia and equipment (i.e., things that are part of the wide level-up system) found in dungeons, something less expected emerges.

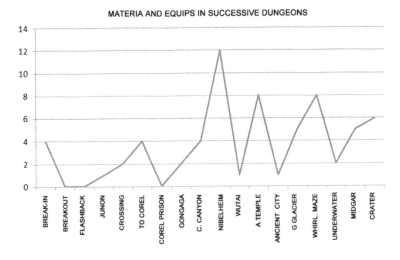

It makes sense that the second half of the game would have more equipment and materia in dungeons since there are not as many new towns to visit and buy equipment in. What's strange is that the increase in equipment and materia in dungeons starts—and peaks— in Nibelheim. Nibelheim isn't a particularly climactic quest. It doesn't sit on the border of a phase change. It is larger than the average quest; there are essentially two dungeons back to back, even if the first one doesn't have an obligatory boss.

Why is this quest so unusually large? For one thing, the Nibelheim quest actually seems to be borrowing a design idea from *Chrono Trigger*: the two-part dungeon. Several dungeons in *Chrono Trigger* have an obvious midpoint where the player can save and rest: The Factory Ruins, the Forest Maze/Reptite Lair, Mount Denadoro, and the Magus Castle.

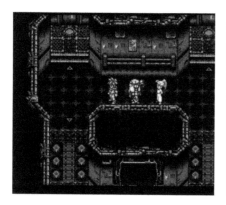

Bringing back design ideas from a game like *Chrono Trigger* isn't that strange; many of the *FFVII* team members worked on it. What it doesn't explain is the changes in loot composition that appear in Nibelheim. Why are materia and equipment such a large proportion of the Nibelheim loot haul when this wasn't the case with most of the previous dungeons?

The explanation of why Nibelheim has so much loot, and so much equipment and materia in particular, is, in a sense, the usual one. Nibelheim probably doesn't have weapon and materia vendors because of the flashback at Kalm. This can seem somewhat counter-intuitive at first, but it does attribute design decisions to storytelling motives, which is always a safe bet in *FFVII*. In the flashback, the player can't be distracted with trying to buy weapons or materia for young Cloud since that would be totally irrelevant to the point of the flashback and would cause some continuity issues in the present. When the player returns to Nibelheim later on, the town has to be reconstructed exactly as it was in the flashback, per Hojo's plan. The thing that makes the later trip to Nibelheim feel so uncanny is that the town is almost exactly as it was five years earlier. If anything significant had changed—like the addition of weapons shops—then the eerie mood would be punctured. This is yet another example of storytelling concerns affecting the design. Nibelheim isn't the only place where this happens, although the other examples are dungeons instead of towns. Corel Prison has no treasure chests in it because it's a prison full of criminals in the middle of the desert; treasure chests wouldn't have anything in them. Similarly, there is very little treasure in the underwater reactor near Junon, even though phase three is otherwise pretty rich in dungeon loot. If there is any explanation other than designer oversight, it's probably that all the other reactors in the game had very little loot in them. Why would the Junon reactor be any different? This is a bizarre example of continuity issues affecting design, but it's totally consistent with what we've seen from *FFVII* in every other aspect of the game.

Towns

Towns in *FFVII* break down into two major types: classical villages designed for convenience and irregular towns that serve the over-arching goal of creating a persuasive setting for the fictional world of *FFVII*. Although the classical villages are also definitely crafted with persuasiveness in mind, we'll see how their primary goal is convenience and speed. I should probably step back at this point and define what I mean by classical village. A classic Squaresoft village is any of the small, rectangular towns that feature two to three shops, an inn, and a handful of NPCs.

Even as the technological limitations on *Final Fantasy* loosened to allow the designers to put in anything they wanted, these features remained. In *FFVII*, we see several examples of this type of village, minus the strict rectangularity. Instead of being laid out in a grid pattern, towns in *FFVII* tend to have a slightly curved shape in several cases. A few other things have changed. Towns in *FFVII* can hold a few more buildings and a few more NPCs than their SNES ancestors. They don't always have more buildings or NPCs, though; towns like Gongaga are more sparsely laid out to reflect the story that the designers want to tell about those places. Nevertheless, the convenience of the SNES village is still available in these more technologically advanced settlements.

In the above image, I have drawn lines perpendicular to each doorway opening and to the town entrance. In each case, there is considerable intersection of these lines in a common area in the center of the town. The overall design seems to be for the sake of convenience and speed.

This neo-classical layout, to term it as such, is indeed very convenient; players can enter and exit a town quickly if that is their goal. For a game that obviously focuses on narrative elements, however, this is a little strange. What about all those lovingly-crafted NPCs? The player has the option of barely noticing them as they fly in and out of towns on their way to the next dungeon. In this case, it seems that the designers prized convenience and player self-direction over authorial storytelling, which is odd since in almost every other part of the game the storytelling is the designers' first concern. I don't mean to claim that all towns are like this, nor that it doesn't make sense in the context of *FFVII* as a whole. The quickness of certain towns makes a little more sense when looking at towns as a part of quest structures. The quick, classical villages are all part of a quest, but none are themselves the site of a quest. Wall Market, Wutai, and Junon—none of which feature the neo-classical layout—all have quests that take place inside the confines of the town. The former two quests are, essentially, scavenger hunts. It makes sense, therefore, that Wall Market and Wutai are spread out across a large area instead of being organized for speedy convenience.

Wall Market also has a much higher number of NPCs than the average town, which makes sense given how many NPCs are necessary to complete the quest. Wutai doesn't have a particularly high number of NPCs, even though it's much larger than Wall Market. This might be a technical decision. The player never has to go to Wutai, so the developers may not have wanted to waste too much time on creating unique NPCs for the town. On the other hand (or perhaps additionally), this could be another result of an emphasis on storytelling. Yuffie remarks that Wutai used to be "more important and way more crowded" before the war, so a large number of NPCs would be inappropriate.

Junon's architecture is still a little inexplicable. The strangest thing about Junon is that it's almost impossible to tell what each building is by looking at their exteriors. There's no logic to their order or placement, so players who are looking for the weapon shop (to use one example) can get frustrated easily.

The camera angle is a little bizarre too. At this angle, all the open buildings have to be clustered near the camera in order to be large enough to notice their entrances at all. This architecture makes sense inasmuch as it helps keep up the pace of the quest. During the quest that starts in Junon, the player has to quickly steer Cloud through a parade, a military drill show, and then get onto a ship. There's not a lot of "leisure" time for the player to spend exploring. In that case, why is there an above-average number of maps and NPCs in Junon? The player can go back to Junon after the quest ends, but there is no in-game indication that this would be a good idea. No NPC remarks the many shops of Junon and how good their wares and deals are. (This is something the designers did do in *FFVI*; NPCs in Albrook tell the player that there are good items to buy in Tzen and Maranda.) The storyline does not bring the party back to (or even near) Junon until much later, and when the game does finally bring the player back to Junon, all the NPC dialogue and shop wares have changed. Most players will never see all that content! If the designers are eschewing traditional town organization in order to make an artistic point (about the hyperbolic, industrial scale of Shinra properties), the design of Junon makes some limited amount of sense. Why is there so much to see and do in Junon if the player is meant to pass through it so quickly? I can come up with no comprehensive answer.

There are other examples of non-traditional town setups which make more sense. Sector Five and Corel, two towns with chaotic and inconvenient architecture, are almost certainly intended to be the way they are in order to make a narrative point through setting. These towns are slums occupied by the cast-offs of Shinra society. The buildings in both of those towns are ramshackle and haphazardly placed. This is exactly what one would expect from the poorest slums. Sector Five is particularly jumbled; no matter how many times I play through the game, I can't remember which of the several unremarkable trailers/sheds contains which shop. North Corel is a little better, as the important merchants have counters right outside the ropeway station.

There is some organization present in these towns as far as shops go; the shops are near an entrance/exit to another screen. These towns are also not as gigantic as Junon, so a little exploration will get the player everywhere he or she needs to go in the town in just a minute or two.

There are also two towns that fall in between the artistic and convenient categories. Both towns in this last grouping are organized for convenience in part, but also have some strange organizational features as well. The first of these is Sector Seven, which has a mostly-standard town area, but that area is isolated far away from the entrance.

Because Sector Seven is the first town, it's impossible to resist the idea that its architectural setup is somehow supposed to be a tutorial. The way that *FFVII* maps work is very different from the way that maps in earlier *FF* titles worked, so perhaps the designers are trying to teach the player about how to navigate them. In the earlier games, the camera always stayed a fixed distance away from the protagonist, and always tracked him or her to the very edge of a map. In the Sector Seven Slums, the camera only tracks Cloud within a very limited area. By placing the shop, inn, and tutorial buildings at the bottom of the Sector Seven map, the designers are able to show how town cameras can be variable (in this case, mostly moving up and down rather than side to side), and that towns are not all on the classical rectangle/semi-grid plan that they were in earlier games. The other town like this is Mideel, which features a central town area that offers convenient shopping, but also has one somewhat inexplicable outlying building.

The westernmost house is a strange one. It's got a shop inside of it (along with a few unimportant NPCs), although that shop is not advertised by anything on the outside. It's not terribly far out of the way, but it's everything that a shop normally *isn't*. Who builds a shop away from the main hub of town and neglects to make any indication that it's a shop? It doesn't make any sense from the perspective of convenience or storytelling, but there it is!

Takeaway Lessons from *FFVII* Map Design

The frustrating thing about map design in *FFVII* is that it's difficult to take away lessons that are applicable to other games. Obviously, there's a clear emphasis on storytelling at the expense of classical RPG design tropes. How can that be applied to other games, though? It's easy to see how the use of debuffs, elemental resistances and component stats in *FFVII* can serve as a guideline for other games—even games that are vastly different. Using the same analytical methods on a much more difficult game like *Shin Megami Tensei: Nocturne* would tell you a lot about how changes to the prevalence of debuffs and elemental resistances, or the strength of component stats, make SMT so much harder. Even if the numbers need to be normalized to be compared, they are still meaningful outside of their own game. There are two lessons that can be carried over from *FFVII's* map design. The first is that the most popular size for a map in a JRPG will probably be one to two screens large. The second lesson that can be carried over to other games is the use of a small number of huge maps to provide context for dungeons. One huge map helps the player to get a better sense of what the dungeon would look and feel like if it actually existed. This is definitely a lesson that contemporary RPG designers could learn from. Games like Skyrim have beautiful open worlds, but, in many cases, the dungeon design seems like a series of unremarkable corridors that belong to a separate and much more mundane world.

Towns and villages structured for convenience in other games can learn something from *FFVII*, but that lesson is hardly unique. Plenty of RPGs have had conveniently structured towns. It is the towns that are structured according to mostly artistic reasons that are especially hard to translate to other games. The overall principle works; if you're making a story-heavy RPG, some of the towns should be designed around story-related ideas rather than convenience. The specific lessons of Sector Six, Junon, Mideel, and North Corel don't give us any consistent, numerically extensible rule that can be used in other games. Designers have to consider the specific nature of each town. Slums should be chaotic and haphazard; industrial dystopias should be hyperbolically massive. How that translates to a game in a different setting is a matter of that setting's specific context.

7. The Design of Towns and Dungeons

8

Music and Design

This chapter deals with the interplay of music and design. Unlike the other chapters, which examined the impact of story on the design of the game, this chapter examines the reverse—the effects of design on music. Many of the various design and development trends that began in *FFIV* culminate in *FFVII*, and the musical trends are no exception. Qualitatively speaking, *FFVII* is the peak of Nobuo Uematsu's second period, which began in *FFIV* and ended in *FFIX*. There are a few primary characteristics of this period. The first characteristic is the prevalence of wind and string instruments playing lines which would be more appropriate as the bass-line of a piece of piano music. Alberti basses and slow, hammering triads played as tutti sections by the winds are two of the more frequent techniques in this style. There are some good examples of this in the *FFVII* main theme. At 1:58 in the theme, the clarinet is playing an Alberti bass while the piano is playing the melody. At 4:22, the middle strings and low brass instruments plunk out three-tone quarter notes that would fit easily and obviously under the fingers of the left hand on a keyboard. I don't want to spend too much time on Uematsu's highly idiosyncratic orchestration techniques because that could easily end up as a whole book unto itself. Such a topic also doesn't really relate to the design of the game in any meaningful way. Other characteristics of his second period are clearly influenced by the structure of the games he wrote for—especially *FFVII*—and so they make for a better topic in this chapter. The other two big characteristics of his style in this period are a heavy use of leitmotif and an idiosyncratic type of introduction whose use he greatly expanded in *FFVII*. Those two features make for a good leaping-off point for discussing *FFVII's* music, especially compared to other games in the series.

One thing I have tried to do in this chapter is to analyze the quantitative aspects of the soundtrack that traditional music theory does not necessarily cover. The foremost reason for doing this is that such an analysis can help game developers who know little or nothing about music. This doesn't mean that such an analysis is simple. For example, to find out how long the soundtrack is in seconds, simply adding up the amount of playing time from the soundtrack listings isn't going to work. Videogame music tends to repeat forever, as long as the player hasn't changed the conditions of the game by progressing to the next level/zone or activating a power-up with its own unique music. In an album form, this infinite loop tends to only repeat twice fully, then fades out on the third repeat. But when trying to count the composed length of the music without counting the loops, it's necessary to listen to the track and stop counting at the beginning of the first repeat. The real "raw" amount of composed music for any given game is the number of seconds before the tracks repeat. You can see these raw totals for *FFVI* through *FFVIII* below.

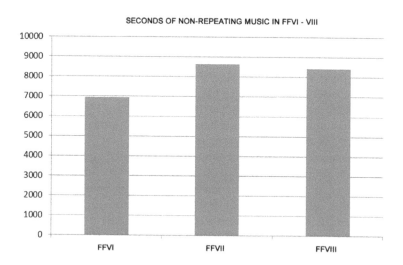

The raw totals speak for themselves; *FFVII's* OST is the longest, but only by about three and a half minutes. It's tempting to say this is because *FFVII* was the game that the original *Final Fantasy* team worked the hardest on, but it may be coincidence. There are plenty of structural reasons why *FFVII* might have more music, and we'll see some of them below.

When counting the raw amounts of music, I ran into an interesting phenomenon that isn't limited to *Final Fantasy*, but is particularly evident in the work of its composer, Nobuo Uematsu. Many videogame tracks repeat endlessly, but they often begin with a few measures of music that are not included in the repeat. This is actually quite similar to the structure of the way that marching bands play marches. When a marching band plays a march, there are almost always repeats of the various sections of that march, but the first few introductory measures are never repeated. Videogames do the same thing, but probably not for the same reasons. Marches feature a large number of repeats because they are primarily composed for a band marching down a street; because they pass new audience members as they walk, nobody notices the repeats. The intro, meanwhile, serves as a great way to transition from a drum cadence to playing music. The intro gives inattentive band members a chance to figure out what march the band is playing and come in on the first measure of the repeated material. It also tends to catch the audience's attention. The repeats and intros solve a lot of practical problems for marching bands, and so their use is preserved in the literature even when bands aren't marching.

Introductions and repeats exist in videogames exist for analogous reasons. The reason for repeating music is obvious; the game disc or cartridge can only hold so much music, so it has to repeat. The original reason for march-like introductions in game music was probably to inform the player that a game had loaded on an old arcade machine. Although there would obviously be action on the screen, players engaged in marathon sessions or who had bent down to put quarters in the cabinet might have a moment's inattention that cost them character lives and/or money. As a part of good UI design, the music can alert the player that a game is starting up. Home console games preserved this feature. The reason this is relevant to *FFVII* is that Uematsu was presented with a problem that he had to solve with music. Starting in *FFVII*, Squaresoft began to use elaborate, lengthy cinema scenes that were sometimes integrated directly into gameplay without a significant pause or break. The cinema scenes, obviously, had to have music. By convention, the section of gameplay after the cinema scene had to have music, too, and that music had to loop. To achieve the same kind of seamlessness that achieved between cinema and gameplay, Uematsu had to musically blend the portions of music that played behind those two things. A good example is the track played over the escape from Shinra HQ.

During the cinematic depicting the breakout from the Shinra building, the first 28 seconds of the music are dynamically quieter and feature fewer instruments. Then, during the actual chase, the music intensifies and stays at a higher level for the whole endless loop.

This longer, tailored intro is what I like to call an "Uematsu intro" because he pioneered their use in longer and more complex situations. I'm not actually covering all intros in videogames with this term, nor am I even saying that every transition into every loop in *FFVII* is an Uematsu intro. An Uematsu intro has two specific characteristics that separate it from other intros. The first characteristic is that the introductory section must be in the same key signature, in the same time signature and at the same tempo as the rest of the piece. It should have two out of those three, at least. Right here, we know that the first music to play during a new game, "Opening – Bombing Mission," is actually two pieces. Everything up to the point where the track starts looping (around 73 seconds) is in a different time signature and tempo. This is probably why that track has two titles (even in Japanese); it's really two pieces, although they blend nicely. By contrast, the first non-looping 20 seconds of "Holding Thoughts in My Heart" are in the same tempo and time signature as the rest of the piece, and really are an Uematsu intro. The second characteristic of an Uematsu intro is a change in dynamics and/or instrumentation. After the intro plays, the looping section tends to be either significantly louder with more instruments or softer with fewer instruments. A good example of this change is the synth voices from "Those Chosen by the Planet." The piece starts with just a tubular bell, low piano keys, and a bass drum. At about 18 seconds into the piece, the synth voices come in and alternate phrases with low synth strings. It's clear that Uematsu was completely conscious of this strategy, too. During the flashback conversation with Sephiroth in the basement of the Shinra Mansion, this effect is demonstrated to great effect.

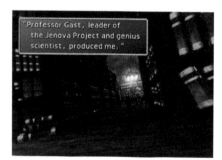 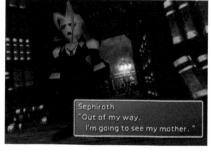

As Cloud speaks to Sephiroth, only the Uematsu intro plays. After Sephiroth leaves the basement, the synth voices and strings come in suddenly. There are many examples in the game of Uematsu employing a similar structure to enhance or reduce the emotional intensity of what's occurring on screen. Uematsu had

8. Music and Design

constraints to work with, but like all the great artists who work on games, he used constraints to produce something amazing.

The reason I point out the Uematsu intro at all is that there's actually a trend in its usage across *FFVI*, *FFVII*, and *FFVIII* that shows how Uematsu had to re-think the use and length of this kind of intro when dealing with cinema scenes. *Final Fantasy VI* actually features more Uematsu intros than either *FFVII* or *FFVIII*, but they're only about three to six seconds long in that game.

UEMATSU INTROS IN FFVI - VIII

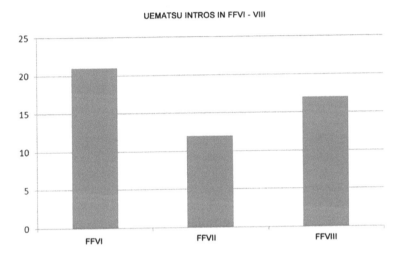

Uematsu only starts using intros of more than 20 seconds in *FFVII*, probably because of the cinema scenes. It seems that because he is dealing with a new length requirement, he actually uses fewer of them in *FFVII* than he does in either *FFVI* or *FFVIII*. That changes in *FFVIII*; some of the intros in that game are more than a minute long—longer than some entire *FFVI* tracks! The reason behind this is almost certainly that cinema scenes keep getting longer across those games. In *FFIX*, the number and length of Uematsu intros actually drops off quite a bit. Whether that is because the use of cinema scenes changed in *FFIX* or because Uematsu was about to enter a new stylistic period is a problem for different book.

Uematsu's use of leitmotif in his second period is one of the ways he was able to turn extremely short musical pieces into meaningful comments upon the plot and characters of the games in which they appear. *Final Fantasy VI* has quite a bit of leitmotif in it, and because that game is focused primarily on its fourteen characters rather than a main plot, Uematsu uses leitmotif to show us sides of those characters which aren't always obvious. (You can read more about this in *Reverse Design: FFVI*.) In *FFVII*, Uematsu works leitmotifs into quite a few tracks, most notably the large fifth-interval jump from the main theme.

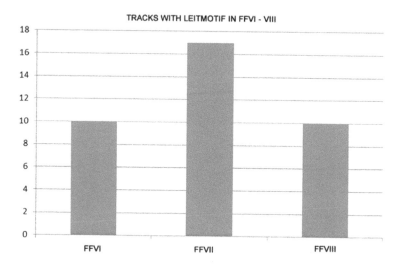

TRACKS WITH LEITMOTIF IN FFVI - VIII

Final Fantasy VII has more leitmotif than either *FFVI* or *FFVIII*. *Final Fantasy VIII*'s drop-off in use of leitmotif is somewhat peculiar, as it represents a total reversal in a strong trend. The use of leitmotif had only really begun in *FFIV*, and only become widespread for the first time in *FFVI*. In *FFVII*, leitmotif is present in almost half the game's tracks. As such, it's unclear why Uematsu backed away from it in *FFVIII*, considering how artfully he'd done it in his past two games. I don't want to psychologize Uematsu—he's probably much more intelligent than I am and certainly a better artist—but there is an explanation I can make that comes out of music theory. The main theme of *FFVII*, which was the most prevalent leitmotif used, is very musically distinct. The motive in question is a succession of three notes in scale order, followed by a jump of a perfect fifth to the leading tone of the scale.

Jumps in melody spanning the interval of a perfect fifth are unremarkable in diatonic music. Jumps from the third note of the scale to its leading tone are not nearly as common as those fifth-intervals to or from the dominant or tonic notes, however. When the listener hears this jump, especially going into that long leading tone, it naturally catches their ear because it of its unusual musical structure. Moreover, the motive only requires one instrument playing it to be recognizable, so Uematsu can sneak it into any track on virtually any instrument. Therefore, it may have simply been easier for Uematsu to work this motive into a large number of tracks in *FFVII* than in other games. If that's the case, then the reason for the large amount of leitmotif in *FFVII* is structural rather than a deliberate artistic decision.

8. Music and Design

Another peculiar thing about *FFVII* compared to the other *FF* titles of the time is its relative lack of diegetic music. Diegetic music simply means music that the characters can hear. In *FFVI* and *FFVIII*, there is quite a bit of diegetic music, and often it's very important to the plot. *Final Fantasy VI* features multiple sections of an opera as part of a minigame. *Final Fantasy VIII* has the song played by Julia, the waltz that Squall and Rinoa dance to, and the music the Sorceress plays for her parade. *Final Fantasy VII* has only one song that is definitely audible to the characters—the march for Rufus's inauguration in Junon. (It's unclear if any of the music in the Gold Saucer is audible to the characters or not.)

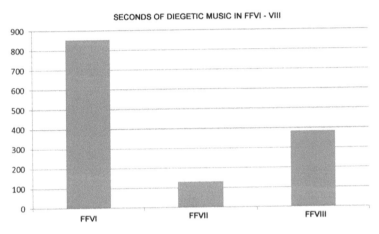

SECONDS OF DIEGETIC MUSIC IN FFVI - VIII

The fact that *FFVII's* OST is still longer while having less diegetic music doesn't necessarily tell us anything about the meaning or artistry of *FFVII*. I do think that the quantitative difference between the totals tell us the qualitative difference between *FFVII* and its sibling games. Because the script calls for its inclusion, diegetic music must be written, and it often has to be written under strict constraints. In some cases, this turns out wonderfully; Uematsu's opera in *FFVI* is one of the all-time great moments in videogame music, and includes possibly the cleverest track ever written for an RPG. Sometimes diegetic music in RPGs is a bit less inspired. The music for the concert minigame in Fisherman's Horizon in *FFVIII* has to be simple to fit the puzzle it belongs to. It also ends up being a little bit bland compared to (for example) the actual location theme for Fisherman's Horizon, which features some of Uematu's best keyboard work.

To look at the quantitative discrepancies between games another way, we can break the music down by the purpose it serves and see how the games differ. Although the soundtracks for *FFVI*, *FFVII*, and *FFVIII* are all definitely a part of Uematsu's second period and are stylistically similar, they have some important practical differences. What I mean by this is that one can place each track from a *Final Fantasy* soundtrack into one of four categories: character music, location music, event music, or battle music. Everything is fairly self-explanatory except for event music. Event music plays during unique events, like special music for cinema sequences and their aftermath, or music denoting non-battle successes or failures, etc.

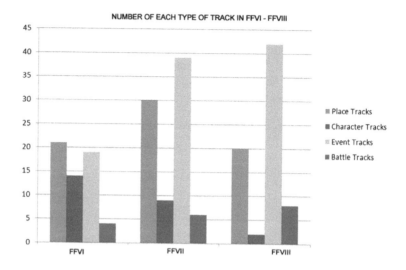

NUMBER OF EACH TYPE OF TRACK IN FFVI - FFVIII

Legend: Place Tracks, Character Tracks, Event Tracks, Battle Tracks

Two really interesting trends should be clear here; the first is that the amount of character-specific music drops across each game. The second trend, more pertinent to this book, is in the abundance of location music in *FFVII*. Chapter 7 showed how much time, care and emphasis the design team put into making the setting of *FFVII* feel persuasive, and the music reflects this focus. I also think that this is a reflection of the main theme of the game. In *FFVII*, most of the major and minor characters (and even many NPCs) are defined by their connection to a place. Thus, the increased number of location themes is also a product of that.

I don't want to entirely neglect qualitative criticism of the music, even if it doesn't relate to the game design directly. The last important characteristic of Uematsu's second period is short but narratively dense tracks. This is different from most videogame music, which tries to capture the feeling of a single moment. This is a very practical approach, as it simply reinforces whatever the director/designer was going for in a given scene. Such a style isn't narrative; it conveys a feeling rather than a story. Uematsu writes plenty of that kind of music too, especially in his location themes. Uematsu also writes themes which encapsulate entire narratives. The best example from the *FFVI* book was Cyan's theme, which shows his transition from cold, guarded discipline to vulnerability and, finally, recovery from his grief. That transition takes a dozen or more hours to play out, but Uematsu captures the whole thing in a two-minute theme, and it's brilliant. Several characters have themes (and reprises) that are very similar to that in *FFVI*, but only one character has anything like that kind of treatment in *FFVII*. Barret's theme is revisited twice, first as "Mark of a Traitor," and then "Mining

8. Music and Design

Town." All three pieces are built around the same pattern of three eighth notes, although the mood of each is very different. "Barret's Theme" is brash, featuring long, major synth-brass chords and a melody that swaggers around the dominant seventh. "Mark of a Traitor" is guarded and hesitant; instead of the major chord progression found in Barret's theme, the underlying chords pace back and forth chromatically. The same three eighth-note pattern repeats, but in a very staccato pattern on plucked strings, meant to show the humble circumstances of his hometown. Finally, "Mining Town" cuts to the heart of the pain and regret that motivate Barret. At 0:58, the ocarina (whistle?) recapitulates the same three-note motive from Barret's theme, but holds out the last melancholy note each time. The music explains to us that Barret's brashness is his most obvious quality, and his regret is apparent, too—but the reason he wants to change the world is because of the vulnerable and melancholy heart he hides from the world. It's amazing to me that Uematsu can wrap up such a penetrating insight about Barret's character—things that we can see but which Barret is too proud to admit about himself—into such an aesthetically neat package. In a mere three pieces centered on a three-note motive, he shows us all the facets of the character he's examining.

Uematsu doesn't really use any other character's theme to tell a story, but the game's main theme is a great example of narrative encapsulation. At the risk of over-interpreting the piece, I think that each section in the main theme corresponds to a section of the game, and Uematsu uses one particular section in a profound way at the game's emotional climax. The early section of the theme (about 0:01 to 0:50) works and reworks the central motive of the piece over and over through various chromatic diminished forms, corresponding to the bleakness of the Midgar landscape. At the 0:51 mark, the central motive makes its first proper, major-key appearance in the strings. The main theme is then developed through the winds, finally culminating in the brass breakthrough at 3:28. This melodic development captures the excitement many of us had as players back in 1997—the feeling that we were exploring a massive and beautifully-rendered world. At 4:00, the main melody is lost completely and replaced by brooding, accented low brass hits and nervous, dissonant strings. This section corresponds to the increasingly dark revelations about Sephiroth's plan and Cloud's self-doubts. This, too, builds and resolves at 5:17, showing Cloud's triumph over his profound delusion.

Just as Cloud removes his helmet to show that he was really at Nibelheim five years previously, the big brass chords of 5:17 of the main theme play. This echoes the triumphant thrill that many of us felt (he really was there!) when we first saw the scene nearly two decades ago. That scene is the key to understanding the score; it shows us what Uematsu was thinking about when he wrote that part of the main theme. From that moment, I extrapolated the rest of my interpretation of the main theme based on techniques he used previously in *FFVI*. I appreciate that there are many other viable interpretations for the music, and I don't want to proscribe those. I do think it would be a shame to overlook one of the best examples of Uematsu's gift for narrative.

9

Conclusion

10 Lessons from FFVII

One of the reasons why I started writing entire books on the classics of videogame design is that I strongly believe there is no shortcut to great game design. That belief makes any end-of-book summary a little bit hypocritical. Nevertheless, I have tried to make a list of the lessons that this book aims to confer, below.

1. Because of the rapid expansion of *D&D*, it's nearly impossible for one game to encompass everything that an RPG can do. Videogame designers, aware of this, have often tried three strategies for dealing with this. They simplify their tabletop source material, combine it with another genre, or they focus all their efforts on just a few parts of the RPG whole. This last strategy is what the *FFVII* team pursued in making their game.

2. Choose your focus and make everything in the game revolve around that focus. Everything in *FFVII* serves the storytelling. Whether it's the battle system, the removal of character classes, the design of towns, or the structure of the level-up system, all parts of the game are made to suit the storytelling. If you aim to make an RPG, you will probably have to make a similar artistic decision (assuming you don't have a gigantic team and nearly unlimited funds).

3. Use game design methods to design your characters along a central theme or idea. The characters of *FFVII* are designed with the same kind of technique that is used in a SNES-era platformer. Every major protagonist and antagonist has the survivor's trio. All the characters have lost the world that defined them, had a near death experience, have something that connects them to their past and motivates them in their quest. The important thing is that these things vary in an iterative way.

4. Understand your medium and genre. Because of the differing structures they have, novels and videogame scripts differ in the way they use dialogue. Expository dialogue is not as essential to *The Great Gatsby* as it is to *FFVII*, because of the narration. Most of the conflict in *FFVII* is actual simulated violence, whereas in *The Great Gatsby* conflict takes the form of short, combative dialogue. Even though these two stories have a lot of thematic overlap, their structural and generic concerns differentiate the way they deliver their narratives.

5. Use NPC dialogue to embellish your theme and world. The designers of *FFVII* put a massive amount of effort into their NPCs, writing more than 1,000 unique pieces of NPC chatter, totalling more than 25,000 words. The two great strengths of NPC dialogue in *FFVII* are to expand upon the setting, and to react to the events of the game. In both cases, they reinforce the theme of outliving the world that defines them.

6. Don't just increase your game's challenge through stat inflation; make changes in the kind of difficulty, too. *Final Fantasy VII* has four phases, each of which offers a qualitatively different kind of difficulty. Stat inflation is a part of the game, but observant players will see how each phase calls for a slightly different strategy because of these qualitative changes.

7. Use a wide level-up system and encourage exploration. *Final Fantasy VII* had to get rid of tactical complexity in order to allow for more story-oriented decisions. They didn't just dumb their game down, though. Instead, they widened their level-up system and rewarded players who explored the many different paths to power in their game.

8. Anything that gives a permanent, periodic increase in power is a level-up. In *FFVII* this includes, equipment, materia, and even limit breaks. These things aren't always equal, either. The items that require the most exploration also tend to be the most powerful.

9. Design your maps with a plan in mind. The designers of *FFVII* made maps for two reasons: to reinforce the persuasiveness of their world, and to serve the player's convenience. These two reasons don't always dovetail nicely. Several towns are very persuasive as settings, but really inconvenient. Sometimes, though, they do manage to accommodate convenience and persuasiveness. The game's signature huge maps almost always have reduced encounter rates and lots of treasure. The

designers want the player to feel the world–not just have to trudge through it.

10. You can't be Nobuo Uematsu, but you can understand some of his techniques. Even among the larger Uematsu oeuvre, the *FFVII* stands out for its length, focus on setting, experimental lyricism, and extensive use of leitmotif. These are techniques you can ask for from your composer! He or she will appreciate your specificity.

References

1. Peterson, Jon. *Playing at the World*. Unreason Press, 2012. (Peterson, 3.1)
2. Mosher, Robert. Nineteenth Century Military War Games: Lieutenant von Reisswitz's Kriegsspiel. http://grogheads.com/?p=3898
3. ibid
4. Peterson, Jon. *Playing at the World*. Unreason Press, 2012. (Peterson, 3.1)
5. Mosher, Robert. Nineteenth Century Military War Games: Lieutenant von Reisswitz's Kriegsspiel. http://grogheads.com/?p=3898
6. Peterson, Jon. *Playing at the World*. Unreason Press, 2012. (Peterson, 3.1.3)
7. Mosher, Robert. Nineteenth Century Military War Games: Lieutenant von Reisswitz's Kriegsspiel. http://grogheads.com/?p=3898
8. Peterson, Jon. *Playing at the World*. Unreason Press, 2012. (Peterson, 1.1)
9. Mosher, Robert. Nineteenth Century Military War Games: Lieutenant von Reisswitz's Kriegsspiel. http://grogheads.com/?p=3898
10. Witwer, Michael. *Empire of Imagination*. Bloomsbury Publishing. New York, USA. 2015, 73–74
11. Witwer, Michael. *Empire of Imagination*. Bloomsbury Publishing. New York, USA. 2015, 63–74
12. Appelcline, Shannon. *Designers & Dragons: Volume 1*. Mongoose Publishing. Swindon UK, October 24, 2011, 9–11
13. Gygax, Gary. Perren, Jeff. *Chainmail: Rules for Medieval Miniatures*. TSR Rules. Lake Geneva, USA. 1979, 16–23
14. Peterson, Jon. *Playing at the World*. Unreason Press, 2012. (Peterson, 1.7)
15. The General: January, 1966. Avalon Hill. Baltimore, USA
16. Adamson, Bisesi, Caparo, Cassidy, Cox, Owen. *Official Final Fantasy VII Strategy Guide*. Brady Publishing. Indianapolis, USA. 1997
17. Gygax, Gary. Perren, Jeff. *Chainmail: Rules for Medieval Miniatures*. TSR Rules. Lake Geneva, USA. 1979, 30

18. Gygax, Gary. *Perren, Jeff. Chainmail: Rules for Medieval Miniatures.* TSR Rules. Lake Geneva, USA. 1979, 22–27

19. ibid

20. Peterson, Jon. *Playing at the World.* Unreason Press, 2012. (Peterson, 1.7)

21. ibid

22. ibid

23. Peterson, Jon. *Playing at the World.* Unreason Press, 2012. (Peterson, 1.10)

24. ibid

25. ibid

26. Gygax, Gary. *The Player's Handbook.* TSR Games. Lake Geneva, USA. 1977

27. Witwer, 126

28. Gygax, Gary. *The Dungeon Master's Guide.* TSR Games. Lake Geneva, USA. 1979

29. Gygax, Gary. *Monster Manual.* TSR Games. Lake Geneva, USA. 1977

30. Gygax, Gary. *The Player's Handbook.* TSR Games. Lake Geneva, USA. 1977

31. Bhodges. Ultima I: The Original. http://www.gamefaqs.com/atari8bit/917775-ultima-i-the-original/faqs/26869

32. Holleman, Patrick. An Intro to Game Design History. http://thegamedesignforum.com/features/GDH_1.html

33. Smith, Harvey. The Dungeon Master: An Interview with Gary Gygax. http://www.gamasutra.com/view/feature/2934/the_dungeon_master_an_interview_.php?print=1

34. Yinza. Final Fantasy VII Complete Script. http://www.yinza.com/Fandom/Script.html

35. Fitzgerald, F. Scott. *The Great Gatsby.* https://ebooks.adelaide.edu.au/f/fitzgerald/f_scott/gatsby/index.html

36. Yinza. Final Fantasy VII Complete Script. http://www.yinza.com/Fandom/Script.html

37. Fitzgerald, F. Scott. *The Great Gatsby.* https://ebooks.adelaide.edu.au/f/fitzgerald/f_scott/gatsby/index.html

38. Yinza. Final Fantasy VII Complete Script. http://www.yinza.com/Fandom/Script.html

39. Fitzgerald, F. Scott. *The Great Gatsby.* https://ebooks.adelaide.edu.au/f/fitzgerald/f_scott/gatsby/index.html

40. Yinza. Final Fantasy VII Complete Script. http://www.yinza.com/Fandom/Script.html

41. Fitzgerald, F. Scott. *The Great Gatsby.* https://ebooks.adelaide.edu.au/f/fitzgerald/f_scott/gatsby/index.html

42. Yinza. Final Fantasy VII Complete Script. http://www.yinza.com/Fandom/Script.html

43. Fitzgerald, F. Scott. *The Great Gatsby.* https://ebooks.adelaide.edu.au/f/fitzgerald/f_scott/gatsby/index.html

44. Holleman, Patrick. *Reverse Design: Final Fantasy VI.* http://thegamedesignforum.com/features/reverse_design_FFVI_2.html

45. Tfergusson. Final Fantasy VII Battle Mechanics. http://www.gamefaqs.com/ps/197341-final-fantasy-vii/faqs/22395

46. Tfergusson. Final Fantasy VII Enemy Mechanics. https://www.gamefaqs.com/ps/197341-final-fantasy-vii/faqs/31903

47. Absolute Steve. Final Fantasy VII FAQ/Walkthrough. http://www.gamefaqs.com/ps/197341-final-fantasy-vii/faqs/45703

48. Xenomic. Final Fantasy VII Item/Materia Locations. http://www.gamefaqs.com/ps/197341-final-fantasy-vii/faqs/42714

49. Tfergusson. Final Fantasy VII Enemy Mechanics. https://www.gamefaqs.com/ps/197341-final-fantasy-vii/faqs/31903

50. Absolute Steve. Final Fantasy VII FAQ/Walkthrough. http://www.gamefaqs.com/ps/197341-final-fantasy-vii/faqs/45703

51. Tfergusson. Final Fantasy VII Battle Mechanics. http://www.gamefaqs.com/ps/197341-final-fantasy-vii/faqs/22395

52. ibid

53. ibid

54. Tfergusson. Final Fantasy VII Battle Mechanics. http://www.gamefaqs.com/ps/197341-final-fantasy-vii/faqs/22395

55. Tfergusson. Final Fantasy VII Enemy Mechanics. https://www.gamefaqs.com/ps/197341-final-fantasy-vii/faqs/31903

56. Tfergusson. Final Fantasy VII Battle Mechanics. http://www.gamefaqs.com/ps/197341-final-fantasy-vii/faqs/22395

57. Tfergusson. Final Fantasy VII Enemy Mechanics. https://www.gamefaqs.com/ps/197341-final-fantasy-vii/faqs/31903

58. Tfergusson. Final Fantasy VII Battle Mechanics. http://www.gamefaqs.com/ps/197341-final-fantasy-vii/faqs/22395

59. Tfergusson. Final Fantasy VII Enemy Mechanics. https://www.gamefaqs.com/ps/197341-final-fantasy-vii/faqs/31903

60. Tfergusson. Final Fantasy VII Battle Mechanics. http://www.gamefaqs.com/ps/197341-final-fantasy-vii/faqs/22395

61. Tfergusson. Final Fantasy VII Enemy Mechanics. https://www.gamefaqs.com/ps/197341-final-fantasy-vii/faqs/31903

62. Tfergusson. Final Fantasy VII Battle Mechanics. http://www.gamefaqs.com/ps/197341-final-fantasy-vii/faqs/22395

63. ibid

64. ibid

65. Tfergusson. Final Fantasy VII Enemy Mechanics. https://www.gamefaqs.com/ps/197341-final-fantasy-vii/faqs/31903

66. Tfergusson. Final Fantasy VII Battle Mechanics. http://www.gamefaqs.com/ps/197341-final-fantasy-vii/faqs/22395

67. Absolute Steve. Final Fantasy VII FAQ/Walkthrough. http://www.gamefaqs.com/ps/197341-final-fantasy-vii/faqs/45703

68. Tfergusson. Final Fantasy VII Battle Mechanics. http://www.gamefaqs.com/ps/197341-final-fantasy-vii/faqs/22395

69. Tfergusson. Final Fantasy VII Enemy Mechanics. https://www.gamefaqs.com/ps/197341-final-fantasy-vii/faqs/31903
70. ibid
71. ibid
72. ibid
73. ibid
74. ibid
75. Aoibhell, Lassarina. Chocobo Racing Prizes. http://www.rpgplace.net/FFVII/misc/chocoboracing.php
76. Adamson, Bisesi, Caparo, Cassidy, Cox, Owen. *Official Final Fantasy VII Strategy Guide*. Brady Publishing. Indianapolis, USA. 1997
77. Absolute Steve. Final Fantasy VII FAQ/Walkthrough. http://www.gamefaqs.com/ps/197341-final-fantasy-vii/faqs/45703
78. Tfergusson. Final Fantasy VII Battle Mechanics. http://www.gamefaqs.com/ps/197341-final-fantasy-vii/faqs/22395
79. ibid
80. ibid
81. Absolute Steve. Final Fantasy VII FAQ/Walkthrough. http://www.gamefaqs.com/ps/197341-final-fantasy-vii/faqs/45703
82. Tfergusson. Final Fantasy VII Battle Mechanics. http://www.gamefaqs.com/ps/197341-final-fantasy-vii/faqs/22395
83. Tfergusson. Final Fantasy VII Enemy Mechanics. https://www.gamefaqs.com/ps/197341-final-fantasy-vii/faqs/31903
84. Absolute Steve. Final Fantasy VII FAQ/Walkthrough. http://www.gamefaqs.com/ps/197341-final-fantasy-vii/faqs/45703

Index